MOTHER TERESA

Merry Christmas Mom,
Peter & Dianne

Lush Gjergji

MOTHER TERESA

Her Life, Her Works

New City Press

Published in the United States by New City Press
206 Skillman Avenue, Brooklyn, New York 11211
©1991 New City Press, New York

First published as *Nena Jone Tereze*
by Drita Publishers, Rr. Leningradi 50, 38230 Ferizai (Yugoslavia)
©1980, 1990 Drita Publishers

Translated by Richard Arnandez from the Italian edition
Madre Teresa
©1983 Editoriale Jaca Book SpA, Milan

Cover design by Nick Cianfarani

Library of Congress Cataloging-in-Publication Data:

Gjergji, Lush.
   [Nena Jone Tereze. English]
   Mother Teresa : her life, her works / Lush Gjergji.
   p. cm.
   Translation from the Italian ed. of: Nena Jone Tereze.
   ISBN 0-911782-88-5 : $8.95
   1. Teresa, Mother, 1910- . 2. Nuns—India—Calcutta—Biography.
3. Calcutta (India)—Biography. 4. Missionaries of Charity—
Biography.   I. Title.
BX4406.5.Z8G5613   1991
271'.97—dc20   90-29004

Printed in the United States of America

Table of Contents

Introduction

To date, much has been written on the life and work of Mother Teresa: books, articles, interviews. Several films, too, have been produced.

As far as I was able, I have followed them with great attention and affection; and they were of much help to me. Still, in all the biographies something was missing: too little was said about her childhood and her spiritual development, her family life, her parents and the environment which gave to the world this extraordinary woman, this sister and mother. As I read the works which deal with her I kept asking myself, "Why is Mother Teresa, Agnes Bojaxhiu, the person she is? Is it just chance that she is an Albanian, born at Skopje? What remains of little Agnes today in Mother Teresa? What importance did her parents have in her spiritual and intellectual maturing, or in her mission?" I wanted to know what influence her childhood had had on what she is today. These questions led me to dig deeper into her life and her works. That was the first reason for the publication of this book: to know Mother Teresa better, beginning with her childhood.

The second reason why I wrote is that Mother Teresa has so worthily and effectively transmitted to humanity the message of love from Jesus Christ, love incarnate. For fifty years she has been bearing witness to that love in India, and now she does so all over the rest of the world. She does it by living entirely for God and for people, especially for those who suffer. She is a wonderful flower in the divine garden, and the greatest gift that our church of Skopje and Prizren has offered to God, to the Catholic Church, and to the whole world, and at the same time she is a marvelous sign of gratitude and of comfort that God has given to us in our time.

By coming to know her we shall know, not only Mother Teresa, her life, her works, and those of her Missionaries, but we shall come to know Jesus Christ, who is the seed of

Christianity and the law of love for God and for our neighbor. Today, like the apostle, she too can say: "Not I live, but Christ lives in me."

Lush Gjergji

Chapter 1
Childhood, Family and Relatives

As the proverb says, the fruit does not fall far from the tree. To understand people's lives one must go back to their roots, to the trunk from which they developed. So long as they are small, fragile seedlings, and until they have waxed strong and spread out their branches towards heaven, not everyone can realize the true greatness which they surprisingly hide and contain. Often, all one can do is to wait patiently. Even the most gigantic trees grow slowly, patiently, without haste or sudden spurts; but they stand up to gales, tempests, ice and hail.

The unfolding of the life of Agnes Bojaxhiu demonstrates the truth of what we have just said; her greatness derives in good measure from the sound root of the Bojaxhiu family, into which she was born on August 27, 1910.

Who were the Bojaxhius? Where did they come from? What did Mother Teresa inherit from them?

To begin with I researched the Bojaxhiu family. Mother Teresa's family name has, according to tradition, three possible origins:

a) some say it comes from the word *bojaxhi* which means housepainter;

b) others claim that the Bojaxhiu family was a warlike family, and for this reason "tinted" with the blood they had shed;

c) still others say that they were merchants, and that among other items they sold paint *boja* = colors.

All three suggestions are partially true, and complement each other.

Origin of the Bojaxhiu family

To obtain as much precise information as possible about Mother Teresa's family, as well as about her life and her early years, I spent a few days in Palermo, Italy, with her brother Lazzaro Bojaxhiu, the only surviving member of the family at the time this book was being written. (He died in May 1981.)

Here is what Lazzaro told me about the origin of the Bojaxhiu family.

"They certainly came from Prizren. But when I was at Skandar, Albania, I found a Bojaxhiu street; and in 1930 I asked an elderly friend of ours (at the time seventy-five years old) where we had come from. This is what she told me: 'The Bojaxhius were a big merchant family, with business interests ranging as far as Egypt. In fact, some of them stayed down there, while others settled in Skandar. A few remained at Prizren, or in other localities, such as, for instance, Skopje.' "

Lazzaro added: "In our family we always thought that we had come from Prizren."

No one knows exactly why this large family moved about so much. Some suppose that the reasons had to do with business, and that the family was looking for newer and larger markets. Others say that it was on account of epidemics, especially that of cholera which in 1850-55 decimated the population of Prizren; or even on account of Turkish persecution, especially the one that occurred in the "Old City" of Prizren (this according to oral traditions).

At that time Skopje was a well-known commercial center. Lazzaro continued: "Fr. Tomex, our parish priest, used to say that our father, soon after his arrival in Skopje, bought a house there. Our paternal grandmother, Cecilia, was in business, like her husband our grandfather Lazzaro. Grandmother Cecilia was exceptionally successful and quite rich; she had a number of people who worked for her, executing embroideries and other feminine tasks, while she saw to the general running of the business. Thus, the family was one with a long merchandising tradition."

Kole Bojaxhiu, Mother Teresa's father

Kole (Nicholas) Bojaxhiu continued the family tradition of commerce. This is how his son Lazzaro speaks of him.

"Our father, Nicholas, was a very well-known businessman. At first he worked with one of the most notable physicians of Skopje who was very fond of him. It is probably for this reason that a number of authors have written that my father was a pharmacist, or druggist, since he worked with a physician and sold medicines. But he was really a businessman and a good contractor. Together with a friend, he was the owner of a very prosperous building contracting firm in Skopje itself. He eventually owned various houses and villas in one of which we lived. As long as he lived, he provided us with a peaceful and pleasant life. He was a very sociable person, so that our house was always open to all. Later, he made the acquaintance of Mr. Morten, probably a Venetian; he was very rich and sold various foodstuffs: oil, sugar, textiles, furs, and so on, what were called in those days colonial products. Papa joined up with him and began to travel a lot, going about all of Europe, so to speak. When he came home he used to get all of us together around him, while he related to us in detail all that he had seen. He also brought many things home for us; but it was especially interesting to listen to him retelling his adventures in his travels. He used to speak mostly with Aga, my older sister, while our mother spoke mostly with me and Agnes.

"Father was a rather stern man, and expected much from us. I remember that when he came home at night he would sometimes wake me up to ask me if I had been good during the day. He questioned me on geometry and on my other scholastic tasks, and always repeated: 'Never forget whose son you are.' With joy I recall how generous my father was. He gave food and money to all in need, without calling attention to it, or bragging about it. Sometimes he sent money, clothing and food for the poor. An eighty-year-old lady used to come to our house; she drank coffee, brandy and ate lunch and dinner at our house. Father used to say: 'Welcome her warmly, and with love.' "

Mother Teresa also remembered her father. "Papa used to

tell me, 'My daughter never accept a mouthful unless it is shared with the others.' "

The Bojaxhiu home was open to all, especially to the poor. This is where young Agnes saw love at work relieving suffering; for her, the first lesson she learned, the first missionary school she attended, was in her own house, and in the bosom of her own family. Because of his business dealings, Kole Bojaxhiu had learned several languages; he spoke Albanian, Serbocroat, Turkish, Italian and French. His circle of friends was not limited to other businessmen, but included patriots also. Lazzaro recalled: "On November 28, 1912, a meeting in our house grouped the leaders of various tribes to celebrate Albania's independence. In the middle of the room they had placed boxes of matches which were then ignited so that the flames reached as high as the ceiling. I was four years old at this time. All night long they talked and sang the songs of the heroes, accompanied by melodies on the traditional mandolin. This took place frequently at our house; Papa helped the patriots financially, and exchanged advice and opinions with them. We once had many photos of these persons. My father was much interested in politics."

The Bojaxhiu family was closely bound up with the Catholic Church. They were close to the Church, not only in a physical sense but in a spiritual one as well. On this Lazzaro relates:

"Our family has been Catholic for many generations. The Church kept us united and helped us. The archbishop of Skopje and later of Skadar often visited us as did also our parish priest. The archbishop was a great preacher, and an outstanding personality. My father was a friend of his, and for this reason helped the Church even more. The archbishop and the parish priest often told him: 'Kole, may the Lord repay you!' Even though my father had to travel so much, I think he was very close to the Church and a convinced Christian."

This is how Mother Teresa described her family: "Ours was a happy family, full of joy, of love, and of happy children. Even though I attended a public school, my family first and then the parish priest gave me a deep, sound religious education."

Kole Bojaxhiu was highly regarded in the city. He was a man with progressive ideas. In those difficult times he sent his children to school, not only his son, Lazzaro, but also his girls, Aga and Agnes. He took part in the public affairs of the city, and served as a communal councilman. One day he went to Belgrade with the other assessors, for a meeting and got home quite ill, returning about eight or nine o'clock that night. With him was the secretary of the Italian consulate. They brought him to the hospital right away, and the next morning he was operated on, but in vain. He died of a hemorrhage the following day. This was in 1919. He was buried at Skopje; a vast number of people took part in the funeral; there was even an official delegation, since he had been a communal councilman, the only Catholic among them. Members of other religions also attended. All the jewelers of the city shut up their shops so as to be able to go to the funeral. All the students in the schools of Skopje received a symbolic handkerchief. (It was a custom to give out such handkerchiefs at funerals; the number distributed indicated the wealth of the deceased and of the family.) This was a great loss for all of us; the house remained without a master, our mother was now a widow, we, the children (none of us were yet grown up) were now orphans. With father's death a man of distinction had disappeared. Together with Mr. Morten he had organized, partially financed and built the first theater in Skopje. We children already took part in the cultural life of the city.

Drana, our mother

When father died the children were still little. The oldest, Aga, father's right hand in his activities, was only fifteen. Lazzaro was eleven, and Agnes eight. This death was a severe trial for all, especially for the mother, Drana Bojaxhiu. On her, therefore now fell the responsibility for work, for the house, for the education of the children. She never stopped, so that the children might still enjoy a peaceful childhood. Mother's maiden name was Bernaj; she came from Prizren. The Bernajs had originally come from Novo Selo; they too were a large, well-established family. "Our grandfather was a businessman and proprietor; he owned much land near Novo Selo. Fr. Kurti,

13

parish priest of Novo Selo, used to ask me: 'Why aren't you interested in all that property?' But my mother, Drana, told me she had no documents establishing her interests in this land, and for this reason she did not bother about it."

"Her main concern was to insure the family's material subsistence. Aga began to take interest in the weaving of cloth when Morten broke off his commercial relationship with us. Mother embroidered, and carried out other various tasks proper to women; she made bridal dresses, and costumes for the various festivals.

"My mother was truly a 'valiant woman,' unshakable, really" Lazzaro tells us. "At the same time, she was gentle, engaging, generous and full of compassion towards the poor. She was also very religious. I think that Agnes resembles her very much. I often noted characteristics and common traits that they shared. She was a serious person, and had a keen sense of discipline. She knew how to keep order in our house, and she brought us up well, with few words, but much good example. She never permitted us to want for anything. I especially remember her strong faith. Every evening we said our prayers together. During May we would go to church for the rosary and benediction."

Like other Christian families they venerated Our Lady of the sanctuary of Letnice, on the slope of Skopje's Black Mountain. The Catholics of our area are brought up from childhood in a devotion to Letnice, which is childlike, yet full of sentiment. Such were also the sentiments of Agnes and of her brother, who even when he lived abroad always kept the unforgettable souvenir of his early years. The pilgrimage to Letnice was the big event of the year, long remembered by most of the faithful.

Lazzaro further tells us: "Every year our mother brought us up to Letnice. Agnes and Aga used to go a month and a half earlier. Agnes was in poor health, and suffered from coughs and malaria; but at Letnice she was completely cured. We also went to Vrnjaca Banja (a summer watering place) during vacation.

"Mother took great care of us. She always told us: 'I will give you anything; ask, and take what you need; but I on my part expect you to be good and show good example to all.' She went to Letnice every year on foot, like a pilgrim. Other people went in groups, singing and praying. We went in a horse-drawn carriage. At Letnice we stayed in some private residence or in one of the rooms in the square facing the parish house. Our deceased father had helped a local man build his house, and in gratitude this man let us use it. We had wonderful times there. We spent the whole day playing and taking walks, especially up by the sources of the river Letnice. In the evening we all gathered around the hearth where we spent the time laughing and telling stories. Agnes always had a book in her hands; mother told Aga not to let her read too much, but to bring her outside to walk and to rest. A lot of people came to Letnice, bearing witness to their faith and to their religion. This included not only Catholics but also people of other religions. Agnes was happy to spend much time in church, especially when there were few people there. She liked to pray by herself. At Letnice we always felt happy; during the entire year the joyful dispositions acquired during the pilgrimage to Letnice stayed with us."

Drana Bojaxhiu was always concerned about the poor. She welcomed all of them, always, and all the time. Both Mother Teresa and Lazzaro remember this very clearly. The former says: "Many poor people of Skopje and the environs knew the way to our door. Never did anyone go away empty-handed. Every day at table something was left for the poor. The first time, I asked my mother, 'Who are they?' and she replied: 'Some are relatives; the others are our own people.' When I grew up I understood that these were the poor people who had nothing, but whom my mother fed."

Lazzaro remembered some special cases: "Lot Gazuri had abandoned his old mother, who was over seventy; and our mother went at least once every week to bring her food, and straighten out her house; sometimes Agnes went with her. I can still recall the example of an alcoholic woman, a really sick person, covered with sores. Mother bathed her and dressed her sores twice a day, brought her food, and took care of her as though she were a baby. Another example: a widow with six children who had to work day and night in spite of her poor health. Our mother took care of her also. When she had no time to go in person she would send Agnes. After the woman died her six children grew up with us as if they had been our brothers and sisters." Drana acted as she did because she felt sure that she was giving to God what she gave to her neighbor. When teaching her own children, in order to make them understand the spirit in which good works should be performed, she used to say, "When you do good, do it as if you were casting a stone into the depth of the sea."

When the children grew up, other problems arose. Lazzaro won a scholarship for study in Austria. Aga attended the commercial school, and Agnes the high school. Lazzaro, the only boy in the family, was the first to leave home. The second trial for the mother was when Agnes expressed a desire to enter the convent. At first, she would not give her consent, not because she did not approve of the idea, but in order to make sure that this was a true vocation, and truly God's will.

Today, Mother Teresa speaks of this as follows: "When I expressed the desire of giving my virginity to God, my mother was reluctant; but at the end she said: 'All right, my daughter, go; but make sure you belong to God and to Christ alone.' Not only God but she as well would have condemned me if I had not worthily followed my vocation. One day she will ask me: 'Daughter, have you lived for God alone?' "

Mother Teresa's early life

Agnes Bojaxhiu was born at Skopje on August 27, 1910. The Christian family in which she saw the light laid the first stone of the spiritual edifice of her existence, of her future life and of her works.

Lazzaro tells us: "She was a normal girl, perhaps a bit shy and introverted. She had many friends, and spent much time with them, for they often visited her. Already in elementary school she showed her inclination for study. She was first in her class, ever ready to help others. I remember that she had a close friend, the daughter of a doctor. Even as a small girl she had a gift for poetry, and wrote some poems and read them to her companions. With them she was very open, whereas with men she was more reserved. However, she was very sociable, and paid no attention to others' religion, tongue, or nationality. I never heard her say no to her parents. Mamma often told me: 'Do like Agnes, even if she is smaller than you.'

"Mother always insisted on order and discipline among us. Every night the three of us, Aga, Agnes and I, in turn, had to polish our shoes. Many times I would ask her, 'Agnes, do it for me, please' and she would answer, 'all right, little brother, I will.' If I had some mischief up my sleeve and she found out about it, she never played the spy. As far as I know, I believe mother felt that Agnes had a religious vocation. I recall that she sometimes said that we would not have long to enjoy Agnes' company, for two reasons: either because of her frail health, or because she would give herself to God. Mother loved Agnes very much, but when God called her, mother offered her to him willingly."

And so, rather unexpectedly, Drana remained alone with Aga. Lazzaro returned to Skopje for the last time in 1924. Agnes was then fourteen. From 1925 to 1939 he was working in Tirana in Albania. In 1928 Agnes entered the convent, and Drana and Aga remained at Skopje. As Lazzaro recalls, in 1932 Aga went to Tirana to live with him. They tried to persuade their mother to join them there too. "I wrote to my mother to take all the personal documents and the titles to our property, and to come and live with me. She got together a few papers, a couple of fine carpets and some embroidery, and in 1934 she arrived at Tirana. When I saw her I ran up to her to embrace her. 'Are you Lazzaro?' she asked. 'Don't you recognize me?' I answered, and then we went home. For me it was the happiest of days, one I never forgot."

Aga had studied economics in Yugoslavia. On returning to Albania she at first worked as a translator from Serbocroat into Albanian, and later served as an announcer on the radio.

In 1939 Lazzaro went to Italy, remained there during and after the war, and finally died there. No one would ever have thought that Drana in the course of her life would have had to separate from her children Agnes and Lazzaro. But, to the very end God asked many sacrifices of this woman, really a martyr, a "patient Job" in Albania. Whenever Lazzaro thinks of his mother he is deeply moved. "Today, when I see Teresa, it seems to me that I see our beloved mother; she is very much like her. When mother came to Tirana I noticed that she was very happy, both because we were all together once more, and because our sister Agnes was a nun. She used to write us often, and strengthened us by her prayers. My mother prayed all the time, in church, at home, in the streets; she always had her rosary in her hand."

The parish of Skopje

Besides her family, the Catholic community of Skopje also had a deep influence over the life and mission of young Agnes. The better to understand the city parish of Skopje, one needs to know the general situation in the bishopric of Skopje, as it was then; since 1914 it has become an archdiocese.

In those days the faithful Catholics were scattered over a wide area, with not enough churches or priests to serve them. Such was the situation as Msgr. Lazar Mjeda, the last archbishop governed the church from 1909 to 1924. To help out the priests in their labors, the archbishop invited the Jesuits to come to Skopje, and for this purpose he turned to the provincial of Venice, who, in 1910, sent priests and brothers of the "flying mission" to open a small house in the city of Skopje. This was made possible thanks to an Albanian priest, a prominent poet and writer, who donated a house for this purpose.

When, in the Fall of 1910 the Serbians reached Skopje, the missionaries had to limit their pastoral action to the city itself.

Things got worse at the outbreak of war in 1914, and they worsened even more with the transfer of Archbishop Mjeda to Skadar, as the new metropolitan archbishop of that place. The government of the diocese of Skopje was then entrusted to his vicar. Realizing the perilous situation of the Church in the area, he decided to ask for more help from abroad. He approached some bishops, various ecclesiastical organizations and religious orders in his own country. He also wrote to the provincial of Zagreb, asking for Jesuits to take over the parish of the Sacred Heart in Skopje. Thus, in 1921, there came to Skopje Fr. Gaspar Zadrima, who was an Albanian. He also spoke Serbocroat, and was thus able to satisfy the many complex needs of the parishioners of that scattered community.

Lazzaro Bojaxhiu remembered this priest well.

"Fr. Zadrima was an austere man, who insisted on order and discipline; but he was also a fine priest and a very hardworking one. I remember that during the religious ceremonies he always held a sort of wand in his hand. I was very much afraid of it. Once Agnes told me, 'I believe you don't like Fr. Zadrima much.' I replied, 'How can I like him, if he keeps that stick in his hand all the time?' She replied, 'You must still love and respect him because he is one of Christ's priests.' "

Later, Fr. Stjepan Cepetic came to help him; this priest was a good organizer. He looked after the children and adolescents, but he encountered a good deal of difficulty because he did not know the Albanian language well. Agnes often acted as his interpreter, especially during the catechism lessons. He organized various activities: games, contests and suchlike. Agnes took part wholeheartedly in these parish undertakings.

Professor Lorenz Antoni too remembers those days. "I can still remember Fr. Jambrekovic. He too was a great organizer and a great friend of the Albanian people."

Fr. Franjo Jambrekovic arrived in Skopje in 1924 to help Fr. Cepetic in the parish, while Fr. Zadrima took care of the faithful dispersed over the outlying territory.

"I remember the words of Fr. Jambrekovic as though it were yesterday. 'Go to school,' he said, 'because without an education you can't do anything.' He taught us all sorts of things. For instance, for three solid months he spoke to us uninterruptedly about Dante Alighieri and his *Inferno*. He instructed us on whatever was of practical use in life: medicine, science, elocution, poetry, and even how to direct an orchestra. He really was a top notch organizer."

"To promote our education and do it more effectively he founded the Congregation of Mary. Agnes joined it and was a very active member. He also set up the association of Catholic youth. This group organized many festivities, cultural occasions, recitals, concerts to raise money for charity, as well as picnics and trips. About forty boys and girls were members. At first, I directed the choir." In a word, he organized the entire cultural and spiritual life of the young Catholics in Skopje.

According to Lorenz Antoni, this zealous apostle gave umbrage to the authorities with his activities, and they decided to get him away from Skopje. No doubt, his work left indelible traces in the youth of Skopje and particularly in young Agnes. Today, she still remembers affectionately her parish and the priests who helped her. Fr. Jambrekovic was also much interested in the missions. In their favor he organized prayers and gathered funds, even though these were modest; and he kept the youngsters aware of what was going on in the missions.

"He used to speak to us a lot about this," says Lorenz Antoni, "or he would read us something about the missions, about the poor and the lepers. He also promoted the religious press, and especially the review *Catholic Missions.* I know that Agnes read these avidly. In this review were articles by various Croat and Slovenian missionaries in India, about the Calcutta area where they worked. I can affirm with certainty that this magazine also aroused Agnes' interest in the missions, and helped to strengthen her vocation."

The two nightingales

Apparently, the whole Bojaxhiu family was musically inclined. Composing and singing, playing instruments and entertaining guests with joyful music . . . these were daily occurrences in Kole Bojaxhiu's home. He himself was interested in music and belonged to a band called "The Voice of the Mountain," as can be seen in photographs dating back to 1912. This no doubt influenced his children, so that both Agnes and Aga were among the best singers in the parish church choir. Lazzaro met Agnes for the last time in 1924, when she was fourteen. "It was a Sunday," he recalled, "Agnes and Aga were getting ready to go to church, and they invited me to go with them and sit in the choir. That day the two of them were to sing solo parts: Aga the alto, and Agnes the soprano. On this occasion I heard them sing together in a duet for the first time. They sang wonderfully well, so that the faithful and the religious declared them, with love and sympathy, the church's 'two nightingales.' " This is confirmed by our noted musician and composer, Lorenz Antoni:

"Agnes sang very well; she had a soprano voice, while Aga sang alto. The two of them performed my first composition, written when I was still in high school. It was entitled: 'On the Hill Near the Lake.' It was performed at a benefit concert for the poor, on March 25, 1928. Similar performances were organized frequently, almost every month. Agnes was punctual for the rehearsals, always arriving ahead of time, always eager and cheerful. She always took part in the performances organized by the Catholic youth group; often she recited, or sang, or played an instrument. I taught her to play the mandolin, which she learned well.

"She was someone around whom others willingly gathered, especially the girls. She was a born organizer. Together with Fr. Jambrekovic she was our inspiration and our leader."

To confirm this, Lorenz Antoni showed me some old programs printed back in those days.

First indications of her vocation

As soon as she had grown up a bit, Agnes began going to church. She was assiduous in doing so from her earliest years. "There was one thing," says her brother Lazzaro, "that she valued more than anything else—the church. We lived quite near to the Catholic church in Skopje, and when we were children the parish priest was an Albanian. Sometimes I thought that mother and the girls lived in church, so devout were they and so willing to give of themselves. Religious songs, the liturgy, and stories about the missions made up the world in which we lived. As long as father lived, our house was a center of political fervor. But after his death we lived more on faith. Mother and the girls were untiring in organizing and carrying out various religious activities."

At this time, while she was in high school, Agnes first felt the call from God. A missionary from India had said: "Everyone has *his road* to follow, and follow it he must." This thought struck her to the heart.

Lazzaro continues: "When I left home Agnes was over thirteen; she had taken to heart the work of the missionaries. When they came home from distant countries she met them and willingly listened to their tales. The priest who had replaced the Albanian priest in our parish one day showed a map in church, on which was marked the location of the missions. This struck Agnes very forcibly. Afterwards, everyone was amazed at her detailed knowledge about every missionary center, its exact location, and the work done there."

She herself declared: "I was still young, perhaps twelve years old, when in our family circle I said for the first time that I wanted to belong wholly to God. I thought this over for six years, and prayed about it. At times it seemed to me that I could not really have a missionary vocation. But at the end I became convinced that God was calling me. In this I got much help from Our Lady of Montenero (Letnice)."

At first, Agnes attended a school taught by nuns. Then she went to the public school and finished her high school at Skopje. During this period she went through much suffering, before she finally came to know what God wanted her to do.

She could still hear in her heart her mother's words: "When you take on a task, do it willingly, otherwise, do not accept it." It was in this manner that the spiritual life she found in her family and then in the parish, and above all the example of her mother and of Fr. Jambrekovic, struck root in the soul of Agnes. She reflected and prayed a long time to come to know what path she should follow. For a time she even strove to free herself from these thoughts, and almost succeeded; but God would not leave her in peace. Before taking the final decision she asked for advice from all those around her in the family, from her mother above all, then from her sister and her friends. One evening (she tells us this herself) she went to her confessor and said to him: "How can I know whether God is really calling me, and to what?" He told her: "You can know by the happiness you feel. If you are glad at the thought that God may be calling you to serve him and your neighbor, this may well be the best proof of your vocation. A deep joy is like the compass which points out the proper direction for your life. One should follow this, even when one is venturing upon a difficult path."

Every year the young Catholics of Skopje and other parishes used to gather about the Shrine of Our Lady of Letnice to celebrate the feast of the Assumption. As we have mentioned, Agnes and her family also went there on this pilgrimage.

Lorenz Antoni tells us that in the two years preceding her entry into the convent, 1927 and 1928, she remained at Letnice a little longer than usual, about two months, performing various spiritual exercises.

When she finally decided to become a missionary in India many people were amazed, while others had expected it. On the feast of the Assumption in 1928 she begged Our Lady of Letnice to bless her before starting on her long journey.

Farewell to Skopje

Her friends wanted to say goodbye and to wish her a happy trip and success in her mission. For this they decided to organize a solemn Easter feast. Today Lorenz Antoni still keeps with fond affection the program where we read in the second part *Goodbye* dedicated to Agnes Bojaxhiu.

When the time finally came for her to leave, in the evening all the young people of the parish gathered to speak, to sing, and to spend a few last hours together, in Drana Bojaxhiu's house. It was a memorable gathering for all, and a sad one especially for Agnes' mother.

No doubt remained. Agnes had been accepted into the Congregation of the Sisters of the Blessed Virgin Mary of Loreto, who worked as missionaries in India. All was ready for the long trip. Concerning this final gathering Lorenz Antoni wrote in his diary: "That evening, September 25, 1928, all of us were gathered in Agnes' house to say goodbye. All brought her some little gift: one a pencil, another a book, or something of the sort, as a souvenir or a 'thank you' token. I gave her a gold fountain pen which she used for a long time. The next day, September 26, was departure day. Many people had come to accompany her: babies, children, almost the entire parish, and her schoolmates as well. All eyes were on her, eyes full of questions and unexpressed doubts; what will become of this girl who is leaving for India, a strange and distant land?

"I woke up early. First, I went to church, and thence to the station. I bought three tickets to Zagreb, for Drana, Aga and Agnes. All of them were weeping at the station, even though a few minutes earlier they had all said they would not cry. I came close to crying myself, thinking that I was losing a relative and a dear friend. As we said goodbye she pressed my hand tightly. I replied rather coldly, to help her overcome the sorrow of this moment. The train pulled out; from the quayside all of us waved our handkerchiefs. She kept on waving until she was lost to sight. The sun illuminated her with its rays; she seemed like the moon which gradually vanishes in the brightness of the dawning day. She finally became an ever diminishing point, still waving, but growing fainter and fainter. Finally she disappeared entirely. Nothing more could be seen; it was like a star vanishing in the blaze of the morning sun."

Chapter 2
A Missionary Vocation

"Go forth from the land of your kinsfolk and from your father's house, to a land that I will show you" (Gn 1).

To India via Ireland

This departure from the railway station was reported as follows in the Zagreb paper *Catholic Missions* in its last issue of 1928: "Agnes Bojaxhiu is an Albanian, born at Skopje. The Lord's call came to her in high school. Just as St. Peter left his nets behind, so did Agnes leave her books behind and departed in God's name. This amazed everybody because she had been the first in her class and was much esteemed by all. She was the soul of the women's Catholic activities, and of the church choir. All felt that with her departure a vacancy would be created. When she left Skopje there were at the station about a hundred people who had come to bid her farewell. All were weeping, and deeply moved."

She tarried at Zagreb for a short while, till October 13, 1928. There, together with Betika Kajnc, she waited to start on her journey to India, a very long and difficult trip in those days, one which involved quite a lot of inconveniences. By train they crossed Austria, Switzerland and France; then by boat they traversed the English Channel, arrived in London, and finally reached Dublin. This was the first stage of the journey. As had been previously arranged, the superior and two Sisters were awaiting them. They remained for a while in a suburb of Dublin called Rathfarnham, where the headquarters of the Sisters of Loretto can still be found. They began learning English, and were initiated into their new life as religious. They took the religious habit and changed names. Agnes received the name of Maria Teresa of the Child Jesus, and her companion that of Mary Magdalen.

There was some red tape involved in getting the required exit visas from the British authorities, but their ship, the *Marcha,* set sail on December 1, for India. The trip was long and very wearisome, especially when the vessel rocked like a baby's cradle, pitching and tossing to and fro. There was not even a single Catholic priest. Only when they stopped at Port Said could they receive communion and enjoy Christ's comforting presence. With them there also travelled three Franciscan missionary Sisters. During this journey toward the land of her dreams, as India then appeared to the young Teresa, they also celebrated Christmas. They improvised a little crib made of cardboard to commemorate Christ's coming to earth. They sang Christmas songs; and then at midnight they joined with the Franciscan Sisters in the *Gloria,* recited the rosary, and ended with the *Adeste Fideles.* On the sea the night was splendid. The moon shone on the sparkling waves. The only fly in the ointment was that they had not been able to attend Mass or receive communion on Christmas day.

We still possess the first letter that Sister Teresa wrote to the editors of *Catholic Missions* from Calcutta, on January 6, 1929.

"On December 27 we reached Colombo. Mr. Scalon, a brother of one of our Sisters, was waiting for us on the dock. We went to the missionary college of St. Joseph, where, in a poor chapel, we gave thanks to the Lord. After that, we proceeded to his house. With amazement we observed the life that unfolded in the streets. Among the crowds we could immediately pick out the Europeans in their elegant clothes from the dark skinned natives with their variously colored apparel. Most of the locals went about half naked. Their skin and hair appeared shiny in the hot sunlight. One could easily see that deep poverty was the lot of most of these people. We felt especially sorry for those who ran on, pulling their little rickshaws, like horses, through the streets. We all resolved that we would never use such means of transportation. But then Mr. Scalon, who was accustomed to these ways, decided to bring us to his house in one of these conveyances. We were all in consternation, and the other Sisters too were amazed; but we had to accept. All we could do was to pray that the load would prove light enough for the human horses. When we got to the house we all felt much happier.

"Over here, nature is really marvelous. The whole city seems like one big garden. Tall palm trees bearing abundant fruit, lift their branches proudly to the sky, and almost every house boasts of beautiful flowering plants. As we beheld all this we prayed that God might in his mercy make their souls even more beautiful than their flowers.

"Next day we went to visit the Sisters of the Good Shepherd, who have a lovely church. Towards 7:30 in the evening when we went back on board ship, we were very happy to meet a Jesuit Catholic priest who was on his way to Darjeeling. So now we can have Mass every day, and life on board ship does not seem quite so empty for us.

"Our New Year's night was not very festive; nevertheless in our hearts we sang the *Te Deum*. Thank God we began the new year well. We had a sung Mass which seemed to be a little more elaborate.

"That evening, late, we arrived at Madras. The coast offered us a melancholy view of these poor people. Next day, when we visited the city, we were deeply struck by the indescribable poverty of these people. A huge number of families live in the streets, along the walled periphery, and even in the most frequented thoroughfares. They spend the day and the night in the open air, on mats which they have woven out of palm leaves, or, in many cases, on the bare ground. Just about all of them go about stark naked. At best, their costume consists of a piece of cloth wrapped around their loins. They wear very finely worked bracelets on their arms and legs, and some sort of ornament hanging from the nose and ears. On their foreheads they bear marks which have some religious meaning.

"As we walked through the streets we met a family gathered around a dead relative, who was wrapped in red rags, while above him were scattered some yellow flowers. His face was streaked with paint of various colors. It was a horrible sight. If people back home could see all this they would certainly not complain over their own misfortunes, but would thank God who has blessed them with such great abundance.

"In a convent where we stopped for a while they told us that there are many Catholics here, but that they are very poor. Even though they don't go about naked they live in very primitive conditions because the missionaries cannot provide them with all they need.

"The city is quite interesting, but it is not as naturally beautiful as Colombo. On January 6 we left the sea and entered the river Ganges, called the 'Sacred River.' Thus we were able to observe a good deal of our new homeland, Bengal. Natural beauty abounds; here and there we saw some lovely homes, and then under the trees there were rows of tents. We were looking forward to living there.

"When the vessel finally tied up we sang a muffled *Te Deum*. On the docks our Indian Sisters were waiting for us, and in their company, with indescribable joy we set foot on the soil of Bengal. In the convent chapel we first of all gave thanks to our Redeemer for having allowed us to reach our destination safely. We shall remain here for a week, and then go to Darjeeling, where we shall remain for the rest of our novitiate. Pray much for us, so that we may become good and courageous missionaries."

They arrived in Darjeeling, where the novitiate was, early in the new year, 1929. After some time spent in preparation, on May 23, 1929, Maria Teresa of the Child Jesus became a novice, and with her Sister Mary Magdalen Kajnc.

The archbishop of Calcutta was present at the ceremony, and during the Mass he gave the homily and presented the religious symbols. On this occasion Sister Teresa wrote to her aunt Maria, the grandmother of Lorenz Antoni, and with this long beautiful letter she also sent a photo. She expressed her happiness over the beginning of her new life dedicated to God. On the photo which still exists, she had written: "Dear Aunt: I am well and my health is good. I am sending you this photo in souvenir of the greatest day of my life, in which I became all Christ's. All my love, from your Agnes, little Teresa of the Child Jesus."

This was a time of preparing and of testing, in view of her future life. She made her first, temporary vows on May 25, 1931, and immediately afterwards she was sent on a mission in Bengal. The Jesuit Janez Udovc, another missionary, wrote to Zagreb about the two new Sisters: "They are really happy and content. I am amazed at how well they look. They already speak English and Indian well, and now they are starting to learn Bengalese, since after they make vows they will be going off to the mission posts."

Missionary life begins

The novitiate, which is a preparation for religious life, is something quite different from the events and surprises found in ordinary people's lives. For the nun this is usually a difficult adjustment, and no doubt this was how it was for young Teresa. She came up against the sufferings and sorrows of a people, and in a manner which she had probably not even imagined. At first, she helped the nurses in a small missionary center. She was very happy in this work, but it did not last very long. We do not know exactly why, but whether it was for reasons of health or for something else, her superiors had her interrupt her activity at the hospital.

The monthly published at Zagreb, *Catholic Missions* in its November 1931 issue, described one of her days in a Bengalese hospital:

"In the pharmacy of the hospital hangs a picture of the Redeemer surrounded by a crowd of sick people; you can read the tragedy of existence written on their faces. Every morning I look at this picture before I begin my work. This glance sums up all that I feel. Jesus, all for you and for souls! Next, I open the door. The little gallery is always crowded with sick, starving, unhappy people. All their eyes are fixed on me with indescribable hope. Mothers hand me their sick babies, just as the people in the picture do. My heart beats with joy; I can keep up your work, O Jesus. I can calm many sorrows; I console and heal, repeating the words of the best Friend of souls. I bring a few of them into the church. It is consoling to see our converts in prayer before the source of love.

"Many have come from afar, walking for as much as three hours. And in what a state they are! They have sores on their ears and feet. Their backs are full of bumps and cavities because of their many ulcers. Many had stayed home, unable to come, too weakened by tropical fevers. One is in the last stages of tuberculosis. Medicine should be given to certain others. It takes a good deal of time to give to all the necessary treatment and advice. I have to explain to them at least three times how to take a certain medicine, and I have to answer the same question at least three times also. These poor people are very uneducated. Now it is the turn of a man of medium stature, with a long black beard and a flattened nose. He winks furtively with his bright eyes, and laughs contentedly under his long mustache. He asks nothing for himself, but with him there is his tiny, graceful wife. Her ears hurt. With haste she is laid on the operating table, to have her ears attended to; for a long time they seem not to have been washed. Our operating table is very simple: it is just a low box which had contained some household goods given to us. Although this is the most common type of seat, that little woman does not know how to get up onto it and sit on it. She stands in front of the box as though it were a monster of some kind; now she raises her right leg, now the left. . . . I tell her again to sit on it, not to try to stand on it! I get nowhere. She does not seem able to resolve the problem. An old man comes to help her. He sits on the box and tells her, 'do like this.' The poor woman had never sat down anywhere save on the ground.

"Other women stood around, or stooped down, waiting anxiously till their children's turn came. What parent's heart would not have worried? The babies' backs are full of boils, as big as your fist. I have to lance them, empty them, and put bandages on them. I busy myself with the task, but just then from a corner I hear the voice of a woman: 'Look, my husband did not want me to come at all, O mother of the Catholics! So I told him I wanted to bring my son to my mother's, and I ran out of the cabin like a crazy woman.'

"I had finished, and was about to close the door when here came another procession.

" 'Where are you good people coming from?'

" 'We come from Belvarave, O mother of the Christians. The people who came here this morning spread the good news throughout the village. Our misfortune has forced us to come and ask for your charity, your love, and your goodness.'

"No doubt, they needed something important, because in India one does not undertake such a journey for nothing. I ordered them to bring me the babies for whom the doctors could do nothing more. For them I have a wonderful medicine. They promise to do so, and keep their promise. I am happy to be able to give them the best possible medicine, baptism, and a happy eternity.

"Later, there arrived a woman with a fractured arm. Then a young fellow who in the course of a fight got a knife in his back from a good for nothing fellow. Finally, there came a man carrying a bundle, from which hung like two dried up branches, the little legs of a chid. The lad is very weak. I can see that he will be going into eternity shortly. I make haste to go for the holy water. The man is afraid that we won't want to keep the boy, and tells me: 'If you people don't want him, I will throw him away somewhere in the grass, and the jackals won't miss him, for sure.' My heart froze. Poor little fellow, so weak, and completely blind to boot. With great pity and love I take the baby in my arms, put him in my apron. The little one has found a second mother. 'Whoever receives one such little child in my name receives me,' said the divine lover of children. This episode of the blind boy was the crowning joy of my weary day's work."

"I was much surprised," says her brother Lazzaro, "when in 1928 I found out that my sister Agnes wanted to become a nun. I had left home several years earlier, and did not imagine what was beginning to take place. Some time later I decided to write to her and ask her how she could become a Sister in our time, whether she knew what she was doing, sacrificing herself definitively. Did she want to bury herself alive? Never will I forget her reply. Meantime I had finished military school in Albania and had become a Second Lieutenant. I was very proud of myself, and very happy. Agnes wrote to me, saying, 'To you it seems something very important to be an officer in the service of a king with two million subjects. Well, I'm an officer too, but I serve the King of the whole world. Which of us two is in the better position?' After thinking it over I came to realize that her decision was not so strange after all.

"Today I tell her: 'You are like me, an officer. You could have finished military school.' It can be truly said that she is a commandant of a unit or of an entire fleet. Her strength of will is unbelievable, like our mother's. She is a convinced Catholic, conscientious and disciplined. This discipline is in Teresa as well as in the whole group of her Missionaries of Charity. It is a very strict order, even down to the least points, with very precise rules. And out there she is the chief."

The teacher

From her childhood she wanted to become a teacher. This was her dream, just as it was for other children. She also wanted to become a writer or a musician, since she loved both these activities and was quite gifted in them. But her call was to the missions. Perhaps she did not dream that in the missions she would become not only a teacher in school, but a teacher of life, in the service of the needy.

After taking her out of the medical center her superiors decided to send her to their college in Calcutta, located in the Entally district. There she completed her studies and obtained her teacher's certificate. Towards 1935 Sister Teresa wrote: "Besides teaching I also have to look after many sick people, and help ten other Sisters in their studies, not to mention preparing for the university examinations myself. I took on another responsibility: the school of St. Teresa, which is also in Calcutta." St. Mary's school was quite far from St. Teresa's and she went every day on foot from one to the other. But this was a very important thing for her, because thus she could see with her own eyes the misery and despair of the Indian metropolis.

Even though she was involved in so many activities she had finally achieved the dream of her youthful days: to be a teacher. It seems that this task was much to her liking. Although it was difficult, she was guided by her great and unconquerable love and by her enthusiasm. At first, the children showed themselves rather cold, as they did with all whites. But little by little she succeeded in drawing to herself pure and innocent hearts among the little ones. Early in 1935 she wrote about her first contacts with the young pupils in the school.

"When they first saw me these little ones asked themselves if I were an evil spirit, or maybe a goddess. For them, everything is black or white. Whoever deals gently with them is adored like one of their divinities, whereas they are afraid of people who are harsh with them, as though they were demons; and they limit themselves to respecting them.

"I rolled up my sleeves, moved everything out of the room, took water and a mop, and began to clean the floor. This surprised them a great deal. They stayed there watching me for a long time, because they had never seen a teacher start a lesson with similar work, especially since in India, cleaning is done by people of inferior castes. Seeing me happy and smiling the girls began to help me, while the boys brought more water. After two hours that untidy room was changed, at least to some extent, into a schoolroom, where everything was spick and span. It was a rather long room, which at one time had served as the chapel; today it is divided into five classrooms.

"When I arrived there were fifty-two children, whereas now there are over three hundred. I also teach in another school, where there are about two hundred more children; but this place resembles a cowshed more than a school. I teach in still another place, a sort of courtyard. When I saw where the children slept and how they ate, my heart almost broke because it is impossible to find more squalid conditions. And yet I was happy. O blessed childhood!

"When we got to know each other better they could not contain themselves for joy. They began dancing and singing around me until I had placed a hand on each of those dirty little heads. From that day on they called me 'Ma,' which means mother. How little it takes to make simple souls happy!

"Mothers bring me their little ones, to bless them. At first I was amazed at this request, but in the missions one has to be ready to do anything, even to give blessings!"

There then began to appear the earliest signs that the promise of her vocation was being fulfilled.

"Go forth from the land of your kinsfolk and from your

father's house to a land that I will show you. . . . I will bless you. You will be a blessing . . . and I will bless those who bless you" (Gn 12:1-3).

She described other encounters with people.

"Every Sunday I visit the poor in the slums of Calcutta. I can't help them because I have nothing, but I go because it makes them happy. Last time at least a score of children were anxiously waiting for their 'Ma.' When they saw me they ran up to me, all hopping about on one leg. In that *pari* (the name they give to their tenements) twelve families live. Each family has one room measuring two meters in length by one and a half in width. The doors are so narrow that I could hardly enter, and the ceiling is so low that one cannot stand upright. To think that for such hovels these poor folk must pay four rupees! If they do not pay on the dot they are put out into the streets. Now I am no longer surprised that my pupils like school so much, and that so many of them have T.B.

"One poor woman had not complained even once of her poverty. I was sad, and yet at the same time happy, seeing how they were made happy by my coming. Another told me: 'O Ma, come back again. Your smile brought sunshine to these houses.'

"On my way home I was thinking: 'Dear God, how easy it is for me to make them happy. Give me the strength always to be the light of their lives so that I may lead them to you.' "

Thus the promise "to be a blessing for them" was confirmed and she could already see the heartening sight of the good done by her activity among the poorest of the poor, as she dedicated her life to them. Time went by. The day when she would pronounce her final vows was approaching, the moment when she would be wedded to her lover for her whole life.

From this period, in 1937, we have these testimonials written in her own hand:

"This happened a short time before I made my final vows. One day a little fellow came to me, pale and sad. He asked me if I would come back to see them, because he had heard that I was going to become 'Mother.' Then he started to cry and told me with tears: 'Oh, don't become a Mother.' I drew him close to me and asked him: 'What is wrong, my boy? Don't be afraid. I will come back, and I will always be your "Ma." ' The little fellow suddenly smiled again, and dashed out into the courtyard, happy."

She also mentioned this other occurrence.

"One day an English gentleman came to visit the school, and was surprised at the great number of children there. In ten large rooms we had 375 of them. It is impossible to imagine what that means. During his visit, absolute silence reigned in the school. The Englishman could not believe this, and asked me what kind of punishments we used to get such order. 'For them, the severest punishment could be for me not to look at them, and to let them do whatever they want without paying attention to them; for then they would be sure that they have displeased me. Why would I strike them? They get enough blows at home!' The gentleman smiled and said: 'The children must really love you, because you love them and at the same time you are working for their good.' "

It was now nine years since Teresa had left Skopje and her homeland. She had hardly noticed how swiftly time had passed, days and months spent in prayer, in work and daily encounters with the poor.

As ever, she wished to prepare herself perfectly for the next step forward, her perpetual vows.

At such times she recalled the words of her mother: "Agnes, when you take on a task, do it willingly, or don't accept it at all." These words were deeply graven in Teresa's heart, and became for her and for her Sisters a rule of life.

She made her final vows at Darjeeling at the end of May, 1937, along with Sister Mary Magdalen Kajnc. Among those present were the mother superior, the archbishop of Calcutta, and many other Sisters. That same year the Belgrade review *Blagovest* (Good News) wrote: "On May 24, 1937, the feast of Mary, help of Christians, Sister Teresa from Skopje made her vows. She has been a missionary in India for nine years."

That same day, Fr. Alojz Demsar, who was still a Jesuit seminarian at Kurseong, wrote to his Provincial in Zagreb, who at that time was Fr. Franjo Jambrekovic, the former parish priest of Skopje, and the spiritual guide of young Agnes:

"Reverend Father Provincial, I have just returned from the parish church of Darjeeling, which is at the same time the chapel of the convent, where our first missionaries, Sr. Teresa Bojaxhiu and Sr. Magdalen Kajnc made their final profession of vows. His Excellency, Archbishop Perier himself officiated. These are the first of our missionaries to take final vows. They are obviously very happy, and you helped them to reach this joyful day since thanks to you Sr. Teresa was able to come to India."

After making her vows she returned to Calcutta. There the Lorettine nuns were well known because of their college and their six high schools. By all they were considered excellent educators. In the eastern section of the city, the area called Entally, they owned a large piece of property. A Protestant gentleman had bequeathed to them a considerable sum of money, with which they had purchased the land, built a Center, and organized a school. At Entally they had an English school with over five hundred girls, and a Bengalese school with two or three hundred students, most of them from middle class families. Sister Teresa was sent there, and with her whole soul she busied herself with the education and instruction of these young Bengalese girls, under the guidance of Mother Cenacle, a Lorettine nun of holy life, who had been born in the island of Mauritius, in the Indian Ocean. At Entally there also existed a Marian Congregation or Sodality for the girls, where there reigned the same spirit which had inspired young Agnes in her native parish in Skopje.

For several years she had taught history and geography, but right after making her vows she was named directress of St. Mary's High School, sometime between 1937 and 1938. She wrote about this to her mother who was still living in Tirana.

"I am sorry not to be with you, but you can be pleased, dear mother, because your little Agnes is very happy. . . . I am living a new life. Our center is a lovely place. I teach, and this is the kind of work I like best. I am also in charge of the whole school, and everyone here loves me."

Her mother answered this letter as follows:

"My dearest daughter, do not forget that you went out there to help the poor. Do you remember old Filja? She is covered

36

with sores, but what bothers her the most is to realize that she is all alone in the world. We do what we can to help her; indeed, the worst thing is not her sores but the fact that she had been forgotten by her family."

The hardships endured by the people in the Indian metropolis and her mother's letter, unsettled Teresa more and more. She felt that she had given enough of herself to the school, after working there for so many years. Her heart was not at peace. Even though she kept busy day and night without sparing herself, faced with misery of all kinds, with death from leprosy and starvation, she became more and more disturbed.

She could not close her eyes or her heart. She could no longer limit herself to the duties entrusted to her by the community. Walking through the city day after day she met many homeless people, dying of starvation in the streets. What had she come to the missions for? Ever more clearly a voice within her resounded: "Your task is to serve the poor."

Chapter 3
A Second Vocation

"Your task is to serve the poor, the poorest of the poor."

About this time Teresa had agreed to take charge of the "Daughters of St. Ann," a diocesan congregation of Indian Sisters who dressed in a blue *sari* (the simple costume worn by the women of the people). These Sisters taught in the elementary schools. Some of the girls she taught, and who often visited the patients in the hospitals, and the beggars in the poorer sections of Calcutta, had told her of their desire to become religious, and to dedicate themselves to helping the abandoned people. All this increased the unrest Teresa had been experiencing; and little by little she began to prepare for fresh decisions.

In July, 1946, she went off to make her retreat. This proved to be the most important journey of her life. On this occasion she received a new call, a "call within a call" as she herself spoke of it to her spiritual guide.

"This is how it happened. On July 10, 1946, I was going by train to Darjeeling, in the Himalaya mountains, when I heard the voice of God."

In almost the same words she several times described to me this happening. Once, during a conversation, I asked her to explain to me how she had thus suddenly and unexpectedly heard the voice of God, while travelling on a noisy train. She smiled and said:

"I was sure that this was the voice of God. I was sure that he was calling me. The message was clear: I must leave the convent to help the poor by going to live among them. This was an order, a task, certainly. I understood what I needed to do, but I did not yet know how to go about it."

While she was telling me this her face shone with gladness, peace, and security. I paused to ask myself, did she have a

38

vision, or an inspiration? Did she hear a voice, or something like that? In the given circumstances, how could she be so sure?

She interrupted my thoughts, and continued:

"The form of the call is not important. It is something between me and God. What is important is that God calls each one in a different way. There is no merit on our part. The important thing is to respond to the call. Just as in that difficult and dramatic moment even now I am sure that this is God's work, not mine. And since it is his work, I knew that the world would benefit by it."

How true this was! I thought of the words of Elizabeth to Mary: "Blessed are you who have believed that what was spoken to you by the Lord would be fulfilled" (Lk 1:45). The Sisters of the community have chosen July 10 as their "inspiration day."

During the entire retreat she prayed and meditated. She was alone with the Lord. Then she spoke to some Sisters of her intention, and her new call. They were quite amazed.

The archbishop of Calcutta too was much surprised who, for reasons of age and of health, had retired for a while to the St. Francis Xavier Institute. Here is what he stated:

"One day I was visiting the convent of Entally. They told me that one of the young Sisters of the convent had some strange ideas. But when someone comes to me with similar accounts I approve with hesitancy, since the hand of God may be involved. If the Sister is humble, obedient and full of zeal, the impulse may be divine. For this reason I gave the person in question full liberty to explain her case."

The archbishop received Sister Teresa with understanding, like a true father. But after listening to her attentively he answered with a decided "No."

Later, she herself commented:

"In truth, I hardly expected a different answer. An archbishop can hardly allow a religious woman, all of a sudden, to found a new order or congregation, as though she had a special divine call."

Every great work of God must pass through difficulties and misunderstandings. Sister Teresa returned to her convent and informed her superior of the negative reply. She continued her religious work as a teacher in the schools. But the same thoughts kept coming back: unceasingly she had her eyes on the poor and the unfortunate. She then consulted the superior general of the order in Ireland. This is the reply she got:

"If this is the will of God, with all my heart I give you permission to go ahead. Be sure that you can count on the affection and esteem of all of us here. And should it ever happen that for whatever reason you wish to come back to us, we will once again welcome you very gladly as our sister."

The reply, then, was positive. But at the end of the letter were the words: "This matter must be referred to Rome."

Not long afterwards Sister Teresa was transferred to Asanol for reasons of health. Archbishop Perier kept her in mind, and asked that she be sent back to Calcutta, because the school was going through a crisis. A certain amount of tension had developed between teachers and students. No sooner had she arrived than Sister Teresa met with all the girls, and went to work to calm things down. In this she succeeded fully.

The archbishop once again consulted Fr. Julien Henry, the expert.

"What do you think of a European Sister who wears a *sari* and wants to take the lead of a group of Bengalese girls, and to devote herself to the care of the poor and the sick with them? Can this succeed? Would people accept this?"

The political situation in those years was very confused, and hardly favorable to such an initiative. In 1947 India had just obtained her independence. Many persons, many political and social groups, and even some members of the government, under the influence of Mr. Gandhi, came to visit the poor quarters, and sought to provoke various socio-humanitarian initiatives. But the step was a risky one, both for Sister Teresa personally, and for the Church which was unwilling to compromise itself in a time of such difficulty.

Fr. Henry replied that in his view this was no doubt a daring step, one which might easily lead to complications. However, the archbishop might permit it, especially if he had the right person to undertake it. The Sister in question would need to work hard to obtain the trust of important people in both the civil and the political spheres; with the poor she would find readier acceptance, for she would conquer them through her kindness and attentions. The archbishop agreed, and allowed Sister to get started.

But this was not the sole difficulty. Others remained. The main one was that Rome, in general, was not in favor of starting new religious congregations, especially of women, because there were already so many of them in existence. Rome sought to deepen the spiritual life of those already existing, so that these nuns might perform with increased conscientiousness the tasks they had already undertaken. To obtain from the Holy See permission for a new religious order, organization or community, the local bishop had to explain the situation clearly; and his approval had to be backed up by sound arguments.

The first condition was that in the locality there were no other Sisters with a similar aim. The archbishop of Calcutta thought it impossible to consider Sister Teresa's request since, as we have mentioned above, there already existed a similar group, the Daughters of Saint Ann, who in obedience to the local bishops, undertook the visiting of the poorest areas, especially on the outskirts of the cities; they wore a *sari* the common dress of Indian women, lived very modestly, like ordinary people, and were Bengalese.

After long reflection the archbishop suggested that Sister Teresa might join forces with this congregation, but she was unwilling to do this. The archbishop at first refused to forward to Rome the request to liberate Sister Teresa from community life in the convent, thus giving her the possibility of working with the poor, not under the control of her superiors, but under the direct supervision of the archbishop himself. Furthermore, it was necessary to find at least ten Sisters with vows, and a few aspirants. All this showed that Sister Teresa did not fulfill the conditions required, and that in addition the political situation, not to mention the Church authorities, was not on her side.

And so, at the very moment, when nobody could help her, she left the convent on her own initiative. She felt she needed to start off from nothing. She could not join up with an organization already in operation, and which was neither European nor Bengalese. She felt the need to work with God in the creation of something new.

Preparation for her second vocation

It was painful to separate from the Lorettine community; but when God calls, every tie must be broken. After receiving the positive reply from Ireland, it was still necessary to forward her request to Rome, this time with the archbishop's recommendation. In her accompanying letter Mother Teresa indicated the first reason for the step she was taking: God is inviting me to leave everything behind, to surrender myself to him and serve the poorest of the poor in the most wretched quarters of the city. The request left Calcutta on February 2, 1948. In Rome it was not attended to very quickly. Perhaps it was presented to Pope Pius XII after some delay. The Pope's permission was granted on April 12, 1948. Sister Teresa was authorized to leave the Lorettines, but would remain bound by the religious vows of poverty, chastity and obedience, which would subject her to the archbishop of Calcutta instead of to her superiors in the convent. The letter took a long time to reach its destination. It arrived on August 7, at the end of the school year. The next day Teresa left the Lorettine college at Entally where she had been working for years. She took off the habit of the congregation and put on a modest *sari* and a pair of simple sandals. On closing the convent door behind her she found herself on the street, alone. She knew what needed to be done, and for whom, but it still was not clear to her how to do it.

She realized that an activity such as the one she was entering on, required much devotedness. Among other things, it called for some solid medical training. The better to prepare herself for her new task, she decided to leave Calcutta for a while, and chose the city of Patna on the middle course of the Ganges. When she spoke of this to Fr. Julien Henry, her acquaintance and collaborator for years past, he wrote in his diary: "On August 16, 1948, Reverend Mother Maria Teresa left St. Mary's in Entally for Patna. In the future she intends to dedicate herself to the poor and abandoned who live in the worst slums of Calcutta. For this undertaking, too difficult for her, she confides completely in the most pure heart of Mary."

At Patna she sought hospitality with the American Medical Missionaries, and enrolled in a course of nursing. The superior, Mother Dengel, was a registered surgeon. She was possessed of a firm character, full of experience and wisdom. Sister Teresa made friends with her, and opened her heart to her about her plans for the future. She asked her advice, and told her one day: "My Sisters and I will live on rice, with a little salt."

"If you want to commit a mortal sin," answered Mother Dengel firmly, "if you want your Sisters to die along with the poor, do that. Do you want to help the poor, sick people, or do you want to die right away along with them? Do you want your young Sisters to perish, or to be healthy and strong so that they can labor for Christ?"

Sister Teresa willingly obeyed this sage advice.

First steps

Having finished the nursing course, and finding herself spiritually refreshed, Mother Teresa came back to Calcutta before Christmas 1948. In her heart she carried with her a burning love, many plans and desires. When she had left the convent of the Lorettines the previous summer, she had only five rupees in her pocket.

Her first steps were to go out and meet people, to visit the poor in their sombre lairs, in their huts, or on the streets. At first they gazed at her with astonishment, even with suspicion, partly because of the way she dressed, partly because of what she did and the work she undertook. Her presence embarrassed them. They asked themselves, who is this woman? what does she want of us? what is she looking for around here? Then, little by little, they were convinced; she was with them because she loved them. This was obvious at every instant, when she caressed the babies, when she helped soothe the

43

sick, cleaned their hovels, washed their clothes, and so on. Their biggest surprise was to find out that she accepted them just as they were, with all her heart and without seeking any personal advantage.

We can imagine how she felt when she happened to meet her ex-Sisters, or other people she knew. Many looked at her with sorrow and compassion. "Poor thing," they seemed to say, "what has become of you? I'm afraid that you will soon end up just like these other wretches." Others wondered at her strength of soul and her courage, and they followed her, timidly, but with sympathy. Some even began to grow enthusiastic over her and her task.

Fr. Julien Henry told the noted Indian journalist, Desmond Doig, how he met her for the first time after her return.

"One day a lady came up to me dressed in a white *sari* with a border. She asked: 'Do you not recognize me?' I looked at her and said, 'I think I must have seen you before, somewhere.' 'Where is Motijhil?' she insisted. I answered, 'You should know that better than I; it is the poverty stricken suburb outside the walls of your convent.' " From that time on they were even more united than ever.

The first school

Mother Teresa began to appear regularly in the suburbs of Calcutta, Tilje and Motijhil. But to work and to help others she herself had to find a place to stay. She sought for one day and night, and never lost courage. At first she rented a cabin, for five rupees. That same day she took in a couple of poverty stricken children and began to teach them. There were no desks, the door would not close, the students had no books, copybooks or book sacks. Worse, they themselves were naked, barefoot, dirty and famished. But their hearts were alive and pure; they were full of good will and eager to become someone or something. Until yesterday they had been cast off by all. Today this unknown lady was working with them. It seemed as though the emaciated faces of these children had in a special way inspired her new task.

For a while she slept with the Little Sisters of the Poor. But sleep was short, because even during the night she went out among the homeless to visit and assist them. Like a night spirit the little woman in the *sari* sought out the abandoned, the dying and the lepers whom she could find everywhere, in the hovels and in the streets. Many had been cast out of the city by the healthy people, out of fear and repugnance. Besides taking care of the abandoned children she also had to contend with leprosy. She had to confront this calamity which people considered as a punishment from God.

But let us go back to the children. Speaking of those times she said: "Those were days of joy and happiness, but also of fatigue, of difficulties and serious trials." This was for her a period of maturing faith, and of growth in her new mission, in a life of renunciation and weariness, in which she could count on God's help alone. This conviction developed as a result of her daily experience, in which God was her only strength and her one resource. It was from this situation that the following prayer emerged:

"O God, you are everything for me. Make use of me as you will. You caused me to leave the convent where I was at least a little useful; now guide me as you wish."

Surveying the unspeakable wretchedness that surrounded her alone, and without any resources, she addressed herself to God:

"O God, if I cannot help these people in their indigence and misfortune, at least let me die with them and near them, so that in this way I may bear witness to your love."

Schoolwork was her first opening, and in this field she felt that she was properly prepared. To the children she taught hygiene, reading, writing and arithmetic; but above all she taught them the divine alphabet: love.

At least one day, one instant. . . .

Her new mission, her "mission within the mission" would not leave her in peace. For her it was as though day and night no longer existed. She was constantly in action, on the move.

45

One day she said to Fr. Celest van Exem, pastor of the church of Our Lady of Sorrows, "If only I could find a house to use as a refuge for these poor little ones, so that they might have a roof over their heads, a place to stretch out their weary members, for one day, even for a moment. If they could at least die like human beings!" She entrusted her problem to God. And all alone she set to work, seeking day and night, until her weary legs no longer wanted to support her.

Fr. van Exem was looking too. One day he went to ask advice of a certain Mr. Michael Gomes, his fellow worker in the Legion of Mary.

"Can you find some way to set up Mother Teresa? Even an adobe hut, or a shanty of some kind? Something simple which would be in the neighborhood? Can you help?"

Michael Gomes relates:

"While we were talking about this, my eight-year-old daughter came along and said to me, 'Daddy, all the rooms in the floor above ours are empty. Nobody lives there. Mother Teresa could come and stay with us.' "

When he had looked the rooms over, Fr. van Exem thought that they were too fancy, and doubted whether he should accept the offer or not. But when Mother Teresa heard that there was a possible solution to her problem she accepted at once, with many thanks.

Mr. Gomes remembered his first meeting with her.

"It was in February. Mother Teresa came with a lady who worked as a servant at St. Mary's school; she was a widow named Charur. But before long Mother Teresa went off again to the suburbs, where her poor people lived. Not only that, but she took my daughter along with her. She needed a lot of medicines. That was how I too began to beg. Once we went into a large pharmacy with a long list. The druggist was very busy. Mother Teresa showed him the list and asked him to give us these medicines gratis. 'Madam,' he told her, 'you came to the wrong door. Let me finish my work.' So both of us sat down, and she began saying her rosary. When the druggist got through he told her: 'Here are three packages of medicine that you need; please consider them as a gift from the company.'

"Besides medicines other things too were in short supply:

46

food, clothes, and so on. It was difficult, but she always appeared calm and sure of herself, intent on doing the work of divine providence. For our family she was a blessing from God. Our house was filled with sick people, the poor, the abandoned. It became a house of new hope and consolation."

Such were the first steps in the new mission. Mother Teresa herself says:

"I washed the babies, who were always filthy. For many this was the first bath they had ever had! I taught them some hygiene, politeness, religion, and reading. The floor was my blackboard. All the children were happy. At first there were only five of them, then their number increased. Those who came regularly received a bar of soap as a prize for their application. At noon I distributed milk to them. Today in that spot there is a modern school with over 5,000 children. There you really see God's hand at work."

In those days she regularly kept a diary. She noted down the most striking happenings, the most intimate encounters. Thus we have an immense fund of spiritual experiences. Here is an extract:

"Today I met X. . . He told me he had nothing to eat. I gave him the money I had for carfare; it was all I had. I came home on foot. I did this for Jesus, and how happy I am!"

A challenge for courageous love

She never was alone in her work, not even in those first days. Sometimes she was accompanied by some former student, or by Gomes' eight-year-old daughter, or some other women, but this last case was not frequent. It was hard for them to take part in such a fatiguing task which yielded neither merit nor money and offered no security at all. It was an audacious venture, but a strange one, full of risk. Yet little by little the circle of her imitators grew wider. One day a former student of hers from St. Mary's, a Bengalese girl, came to pay her a visit. Mother Teresa was surprised; for a long time they gazed into each other's eyes. Then the girl, deeply moved, found her voice. "Mother," she said, "I came to live with you."

47

Mother Teresa, calm and gently smiling, showed the girl her hands and her habit, the ramshackle house, and the poor people in it, without saying a word. Finally she spoke: "Very well, my daughter, you see my hands and my clothes; compare them with yours. Religious life, especially this kind of religious life, demands in a high degree the spirit of sacrifice. A nun must first of all forget herself, to dedicate herself to God and her neighbor."

The girl replied: "I understand; I have thought about it for a long time. I'm ready. I beg you to accept me."

To test this vocation Mother Teresa did not refuse the girl outright, but told her to come back later, after some time. She remembered her own long drawn out path which she had had to follow: six years for her first vocation, and so many more for the second.

On St. Joseph's day, March 19, 1949, Mother Teresa was praying in the chapel when a knock sounded on the door. When she opened it she saw the young girl, simply dressed, wearing no jewelry. Her family was quite well-to-do. For her it was a real event: getting rid of her beautiful clothes and ornaments. This indicated that she really wanted to walk in the path of sacrifice for others.

"Here I am, Mother Teresa," she said; "I have come as you told me. I beg you not to refuse me this time. I have fully made up my mind."

This was the first vocation, the first member of the Company of the Sisters of Charity. Today she is called Sister Agnes. Out of respect she took the baptismal name of Mother Teresa: Agnes. And Mother Teresa never forgot that Agnes was the first to believe in the spirit of the new way of life.

Gradually the number of Sisters increased. In May of that same year Mother Teresa wrote to a friend in Europe: "I now have three Sisters, all of them very dedicated. There is so much suffering, so much need for God among the people, and we are so few to help them! If you could only see how faces light up when they meet the Sisters. Pray to Our Lady to send us more Sisters. If we had twenty here in Calcutta, there would be plenty of work for all."

In November 1949, she wrote: "Now we are five. Pray much

so that our community may grow in holiness and numbers, if such is God's will. There is so much to do."

Laboring as she did day and night, without yielding before any difficulty, she attracted the attention of many people. At first only a few volunteers came, mainly from among her former students, but some were doctors, professors, parents. . . . Thus her community grew little by little. She called it that rather than "company." Once she told me, on this subject:

"We really are not an order, nor a 'company,' but a community, a family. Otherwise how could we hold out in a task so demanding, scattered as we are about the world, constantly laboring in the streets, the schools, the hospitals?"

By the next year, 1950, they were seven including Sister Mary, the first recruit from Bangladesh. Mother Teresa instructed them by her words, but even more by her example.

The first rule

It was becoming clear that a new congregation had been started. To be recognized as such it needed a rule which would then have to be sent to Rome for approval. Thus there arose the problem of how to incorporate their experience in the proper form and to explain it in terms of Canon Law. In this too she found excellent advisers.

Here we must mention two names we have already met: Father Julien Henry, and Father Celest van Exem, both Belgians.

Who wrote the rule?

The first sketch was written by Mother Teresa herself, explaining her principles and spiritual goals. As for the legislative and organizational sections, Fr. van Exem helped her a great deal. At the beginning, Mother Teresa wanted her Sisters not to own anything, not even buildings. She would have wanted everything to belong to the Church. But this was not possible, since the Catholic Church and the Vatican were foreign entities in India.

After working together for a long time on the project, they put the rules into the hands of Fr. de Gheldere for the final revision. At the end he declared: "The finger of God is here."

The original title of the rule was in English: "Constitutions of the Society of the Missionaries of Charity."

It was the fruit of experience and of a new and specific style of work.

At the outset the following was immediately made plain: "Our aim is to quench the great thirst of the love of Jesus Christ by our evangelical vows, to dedicate ourselves freely to serving the poorest of the poor according to the example and the teaching of our Lord, and thus to proclaim in a special way the kingdom of God.

"Our specific mission is to work for the salvation and the sanctification of the poorest of the poor.

"As Jesus was sent by the Father, so too he sends us, filled with his Spirit, to proclaim the gospel of his love, his compassion for the poorest of the poor in the whole world. Our specific mission is to proclaim Jesus Christ to the people of all nations, especially those confided to our care.

"We are called Missionaries of Charity.

"God is love. The missionary must be a missionary of love. Her soul must be full of love and she should communicate it to the souls of others, be they Christians or not."

Laying down the essential points in such clear light impresses us. It reminds us of the other great founders and foundresses of orders in the history of the church: St. Basil, St. Benedict, St. Francis, St. Ignatius . . .

Archbishop Perier of Calcutta, sent the rule to Rome for approval in 1950. He had to wait for several months before receiving a reply. This arrived at the beginning of autumn. Pope Pius XII, through the Congregation of Religious, approved the foundation of the Company of the Missionaries of Charity, established in Calcutta, #14, Greek Lane.

On October 7, feast of Our Lady of the Rosary, in the Sisters' chapel the archbishop celebrated Mass, during which Fr. van Exem read the papal bull of foundation. On that same day every year, the anniversary of the company is celebrated. At that time there were twelve Sisters, an encouraging number.

Here is their daily schedule: Rising at 4:30; at 5:00 prayers; at 5:45 Mass with homily even on ordinary days. Then breakfast and clean up time. From 8:00 to 12:30, work for the poor and needy. At 12:30, lunch followed by a short rest period. At 2:30, spiritual reading and meditation until 3:00, followed by tea; from 3:15 to 4:30 adoration of the Most Blessed Sacrament. Then more work for the poor till 7:30, after which, dinner; at 9:00 night prayer; 9:45 bedtime.

The entire regulation was based on a single principle: love for God and for one's neighbor: being ever ready to serve the suffering, the most needy, the poorest of the poor.

Another house

The number of the poor and sick kept on increasing. In 1953 it became necessary to find a larger house in which to gather and instruct the new recruits who flocked in hoping to dedicate themselves to missionary life. Money to buy such a house was, of course, non-existent. Times were hard everywhere, especially in India.

Mother Teresa made a novena to St. Cecilia, relates Fr. Julien Henry, who on this occasion also proved her faithful ally. Just then a Muslim who was moving to Pakistan had put his house up for sale. Fr. Julien went to see him and was cordially received. When asked how much he wanted for the building, he asked Father to make him an offer. The latter suggested a *Lakh* (7,500 pounds sterling) which was precisely the cost price. Archbishop Perier, who had just undergone an operation on the retina, understood the urgent nature of the case, and gave his consent. Within three days the purchase of the house was concluded. When Mother Teresa came to inspect the premises she objected: "Father, this is too big; what shall we do with all this empty space?"

"It will all be used," answered the missionary. "In fact the day will come when you will ask where to put all those who come to you." Indeed, this was not one house, but three, in a splendid location in the center of the city. And so it was that a Muslim's property became the mother house of the Missionaries of Charity in Calcutta (54A Lower Circular Road).

The Sisters' community kept on growing. Their modest

lifestyle and the spirit of sacrifice with which they worked in the streets, in the hovels, and in the poorest sections of the city won for them the deepest esteem and sympathy on the part of the population. The barriers of distrust crumbled. Bishops, priests, Sisters of other congregations, ordinary people, many men and women of various religions, classes and origins began coming to offer their help.

The first novitiate

Mother Teresa's constancy and that of her first Sisters was rewarded by more vocations. The first ones came from Calcutta and the surrounding area, and then from other parts of India. Today they come from all over the world. Because they had been matured in mission work and in spirituality, in daily labor and in their common life, the Sisters were always ready to welcome new co-workers. Thus, almost spontaneously, the first novitiate took shape. Mother Teresa was the first guide and directress. To help her in the spiritual formation of her Sisters she found a priest to act as spiritual father, and from the beginning she made clear to him the limitations of his role:

"Please do not interfere with the internal running of the house. As you know, some priests would like for me to change some points of the rule. For instance, they have told me that we should have curtains on the windows of our common room. I don't want any. The poor whom we serve don't have any. Most of our Sisters come from farmhouses where they didn't have any either. They should not live more commodiously here than they did at home. So, I beg you, do not try to interfere."

In dealing with priests she was clear and firm. She highly respected their role and their cooperation, but she did not permit them any interference with the life of the community. All difficulties, conflicts or problems that arose had to be resolved first of all within the community itself, with the collaboration of all the Sisters; and only if there was no other way of resolving them could the external help of someone else be asked for.

In this connection she once told us at a conference she gave at Oslo: "Many times my Sisters commit two mistakes. Either they do not permit anyone to guide them, and so they remain closed in on themselves; or they open themselves too much, completely, thus allowing anybody to interfere in their interior life, something that does not occur without bringing with it unfortunate consequences. Both these ways of acting are mistaken. The hardest thing in life is to maintain one's balance."

The first confessor who had much influence over the Sisters' community life was Fr. Edward Le Loly, a Jesuit missionary from Belgium. He published a book on Mother Teresa, entitled *We do it for Jesus: Mother Teresa and Her Missionaries of Charity* (London, 1977). This is one of the best studies about her which has come out so far. Much of the information found in this present book was taken from Fr. Le Loly's.

When Fr. Edward began confessing the novices there were thirty-five girls in the community. The following year there were fifty, then seventy and more. In 1963 Mother Teresa wrote to the seminarians of the diocese of Skopje who were studying at Zagreb a letter which she began in English, and continued in Albanian:

"I received your letter and thank you for your prayers which help me to pursue the work of God. I am happy that you are preparing to labor at Skopje. Do not forget that the Lord has called and chosen you so that you may become one great family which should fill your hearts. We are now 181 Sisters, and we have begun to work with men too, our Brothers.

"I've forgotten much of my Albanian, and so cannot write to you at greater length. Pray for me, and I shall pray for you. May God's love embrace you all. Mother Teresa, M.C."

With the growing number, the work too became heavier; then Mother Teresa named Sister Agnes to be the guide and directress of the novices, and Sister Federica her assistant. The increase in vocations was a blessing, but much experience was needed to insure a true and harmonious development of these new recruits.

This large influx of vocations at the beginning could have

been perilous. The danger was that the primitive spirit might have been diluted. To the Sisters in charge Mother Teresa taught what she is still repeating today: "Our growth is something beautiful and promises much success; but two things must be understood: this progress must proceed qualitatively and quantitatively, along with the mystical life of holiness."

"One evening two Sisters brought two sick women to the house. One of them was suffering very much; her body was covered with wounds and vermin. I cleaned her up and put her in a bed. She took my hand, and her face lighted up with joy, like that of an angel. She smiled, content. She had time to say only one word to me: 'Thank you!' and then she died. This poor sick woman gave me much more than I had given her. She gave me love, with gratitude. At that moment I asked myself what I would have told her had I been in her place and she in mine. Probably, 'I'm hungry,' or something of the sort, to attract to myself the attention, the charity and the pity of others. But she, on the contrary, gave me much." (Mother Teresa speaking at Skopje, March 28, 1978.)

To be closer to the poor Mother Teresa wished to live with them and like them. For this reason she chose to wear the *sari,* the costume of poor Indian women. "The *sari* makes it possible for our Sisters to feel themselves poor among the poor, on a level with the sick, the children, the aged . . . Thus our manner of dressing brings us closer to their life."

Chapter 4
For the Poorest of the Poor

Caring for the poor and the sick

Every day in the world there are many hungry people, the sick, the lepers. . . . Some are born in the street, live outdoors without ever knowing what it is to have a roof over their heads. They are buried at the end, without ever having lived a single happy day.

Facing such distress, we remain unmoved. Perhaps for a moment or two we become thoughtful; but then we ask ourselves: what can I do to cope with so much misery, inequality and poverty? My efforts can't change anything. What difference could I make? All I might do is to wear myself out, and for what? Fate is fate. May God help them somehow!

The world will never go right as long as it is divided into the rich and the poor. The rich get richer, and the poor get poorer, and neither group has any way of changing this situation.

Mother Teresa confronted this agonizing problem from the moment she set foot on the soil of Asia, at Colombo, at Madras, and especially at Calcutta. How often must she not have asked herself: What can I do, a mere nun, a stranger, if those far more important and influential than I can do so little? In some respects Mother Teresa resembles the prophet Jonas in the Old Testament. Unexpectedly, she too found herself all alone, facing a whole world of poverty stricken and desperate people.

When she left the convent she wrote in her diary:

"I get the impression that I am living through a shipwreck in an ocean of sorrow and despair. The Lord wanted me to be a Sister free to act, wearing the cross on my mantle. But today I got a good lesson. Poverty is hard for the poor to bear. I wanted a place where I could shelter the most needy. To find one I walked and walked, till I was exhausted. My hands and legs trembled with fatigue. I finally understood how soul and body suffer among the poor when they have to look for shelter, food and medicine. I can't forget how easy everything was in the convent. This is a temptation."

Should she stay or go back? She wanted to stay and work. But, what did she need to do, and where should she begin?

The Voice said to her: "Go, and serve the poorest of the poor without any distinction of classes or faith. Serve them, and in them recognize God who is suffering. Look for the poor in the streets and squares, the sidewalks, the caverns and the rundown quarters of the city. Be with them day and night, among them, and for them, in spite of their unspeakable misery, even death itself."

This little woman, meanly dressed, with small hands and burning eyes but with a large, pure heart filled with living faith and trust in the Lord, plunged into these problems and faced them in order to conquer them. Henceforth her watchword was: "No one should leave me without feeling better and happier. For the sick I must be the ray of God's goodness, ever ready to smile at the children whom I gather up and help, for all the rejected ones, for all those whom I love and serve and whom I keep company with. I should give far too little if I handed out medicine only, and not my heart."

She forged ahead, and studied the situation patiently. Thus, she accumulated experience.

"We are not social workers. We want to bring our people both happiness and divine love, God himself who loves them through us. Thus we love God by serving him through them.

"There are many organizations that tend the sick. We are not among them. We are not social uplifters. We must be more than that; we must give more than that; we must give of ourselves, and with this attitude we can impart the love of God. The poor have helped us to discover what it means to love and serve God; it is something that we shall discover and really understand only in heaven."

At Oslo she said, among other things: "Even though they are extremely poor, our people die happy, for they are free. That is where true happiness resides. Let us all pray together today so that God may give peace to the world through those who are suffering" (December 9, 1971).

Her philosophy, or her world view, has the novelty of this unexpected notion: the poor give to the Sisters much more than they receive from them.

Which is why the Missionaries of Charity, besides the usual three vows of poverty, chastity and obedience, make a fourth vow: "service to the poorest of the poor," giving their lives freely to the poorest, with all their hearts.

The poor! This tribe of poverty! Today the world calls her "the mother of the poor." She is the hope of the poor all over the world. They believe, they hope, even when there is no hope, like Abraham.

Mother Teresa's Sisters, like all her achievements (houses for the sick, for the lepers, for the dying, for babies and old folks), are all founded on faith in God.

"We do not receive any regular support from the government. We have no specific revenues. All we have is the certainty of our trust in God. He is concerned about the flowers of the field, about the birds, about the grass that grows all over the world. He will also take care of our poor people."

Once the Sacred Congregation of *Propaganda Fide* (today the Congregation for the Evangalization of Peoples) which has control over certain dioceses of Yugoslavia, among others those of Skopje and Prizren, decided to give her a subsidy of $25,000 every three months to provide for the Sisters' needs, and especially for the upkeep of the Novitiate in India—at the time there were one hundred novices there. But Mother Teresa refused the money, saying:

"I do not want any material security for our Sisters. We do not want to have any bank accounts, or any assured means of subsistence. We must proceed with hope in divine Providence. The greatest danger we could encounter would be to get rich." Some time later, the same Sacred Congregation sent her another subsidy, but this time it was neither for the Sisters nor for the Novitiate, but for the poor and especially the lepers. Mother Teresa gratefully accepted this donation.

This is her manner of living: "We need poverty if we are to live free, both materially and spiritually. We need such

57

freedom, a freedom like the one we find in those around us, so as not to become enslaved by wealth. Nobody can oblige us to enrich ourselves. We must consecrate ourselves exclusively to poverty. Christ chose liberty. If we truly want to belong to Christ, then we must be poor."

The house for the dying

When visiting the poor, Mother Teresa came across many desperate situations. Every day she beheld people who were destined to die in the streets. From afar she could hear their lamentations. She stopped before them and her Voice said to her, "Help them! At least let them die like human beings." So she established at Calcutta the first refuge for the dying. This is the well-known *Nirmal Hriday* (Pure Heart) refuge, opened in 1954 at #14 Creek Lane.

On one occasion she said: "Our life is bound up with that of Jesus by means of holy communion. We receive Jesus under the appearance of bread; we must also recognize him in those around us, in others, in all people, in the poor and forsaken.

"Our meeting with Jesus in communion should prepare us to recognize and serve him in our neighbor, for Jesus himself said: 'What you do to the least of my brothers, you do to me,' 'I was rejected, and you took me in.' "

As Miguel Gomes relates, it all started like this:

"One day we found a dying man by the sidewalk, not far from Campbell Hospital, near our house. Mother Teresa went to the hospital to ask admission for this poor wretch. In vain. No room for him there. We went to a pharmacy to get some medicine, but when we returned he was already dead. Deeply moved, she said: 'They take better care of their cats and dogs than of human beings.' And with that she went to protest to the authorities."

That was when a house for the dying was opened at Kalighatu. Some writers have said that Mother Teresa found an old woman covered with sores lying on the ground; the mice were already starting to bite her. Such cases were not exceptional. So she sought a place for these people. With this in mind she visited some buildings near the temple of Kali, the protectress of Calcutta, which the pilgrims used as shelters. Acknowledging that there was a real emergency to be faced, the authorities gave her permission to use these buildings for a while, until something better could be devised. The joy of the poor people was great. But opposition soon surfaced, especially from the representatives of the young Hindus; they could not accept the idea that in their religious center a Catholic refuge should be established. They incited politicians against Mother Teresa, and protested against this "stranger" who was trying to proselytize the poor. A certain eminent personage interested himself in this affair and promised the representatives of the Hindus and other enemies of Mother Teresa that he would make her vacate the premises. Thus, one day he came to pay her a visit. She showed him through rooms crowded with people in the most horrible conditions. When with his own eyes he had seen their misery and also the love and tenderness shown by the Sisters, he remained speechless. Although he had come in anger, determined to make the Sisters leave, he changed his mind, overcome by what he had seen. He approached Mother Teresa, took her hand to congratulate her, and said: "Keep on with your work. I wish you good luck and success. May God help you!"

On leaving the premises he said to the journalists present:

"Yes, I did promise to send this woman away; and I am ready to maintain my word; but pay attention to what I am about to tell you: before that happens, your mothers and sisters and you yourselves must come here and do what these Sisters are doing. In the temple over there you have a goddess made of black stone; here you have a goddess who is alive."

Sometimes the police helped the Sisters. When they found people lying prostrate in the streets they notified Mother Teresa, and brought these wretches to her. First of all the Sisters bathed them carefully, put clean clothes on them, then put them to bed. For them this was the start of a new life. They even found medical attention, something that up to then they had never even imagined.

For this activity the Missionaries of Charity received another house, in 1975, donated by the local authorities.

Today Mother Teresa has a vast organization, with buildings convalescent houses, vehicles, medical men and nurses, thousands of friends, co-workers and benefactors all over the world. At first it was certainly not like that, when she had to struggle against difficulties which put her to the test, and she had to resist entrenched opposition.

In a conversation with Mother Teresa at Oslo, she was asked whether the Sisters had cars or other means of transportation, and how they got from place to place. She answered:

"No, the Sisters have no personal means of transportation, which belong to us. In fact, we don't even have a private life of our own; our life is lived in common with the poor, But we do use vehicles and ambulances for the sick and the poor.

"Here is how I got our first ambulance. An American priest had been saving the money given him for Mass intentions, and with it he bought the vehicle, then sent it to us to use for our sick. This gesture made us very happy. We were amazed at the kindness of this poor priest who, for years, with love and prayers had been following our work. This gave us even more courage."

In carrying out this particularly exhausting activity the male component of the Company, called Missionary Brothers of Charity, which Mother Teresa founded in 1963, has been of very great importance.

Houses for abandoned children and orphans

"We always have a place ready, and a bed, even for a single child."

From the very beginning, one of the most difficult problems faced by the Company was that of providing for the babies, especially those with no parents: the unwanted ones, the unloved ones, the children of separated parents. The world today is full of such infants. In India, as in the rest of the world, there are many hungry children; but in addition another current and very painful problem, a worldwide problem, is that of the handicapped, the physically or mentally deficient ones.

After some time Mother Teresa opened an asylum for abandoned and orphaned children. She called it the *Children's Home*. This was in 1955. There she gathered babies abandoned almost as soon as they were born, the sick ones, the poor ones, the unwanted ones. Such infants were picked up in the darkest streets of the city, often in garbage heaps where they had simply been thrown away. Sometimes the mothers themselves brought these poor innocents to her.

Today Mother Teresa declares with a certain pride and with the greatest joy: "Up to now we have never turned away any person, any child. We always have a place ready, a bed for one more."

In Oslo, discussing this problem, Mother Teresa said: "This prize came just at the right moment, because we have many young people who want to get married but cannot do so because they don't have any dwelling. We shall manage to provide all of them with a house of their own."

On that occasion, Bishop Nikola Prela gave her the rosary that Pope Paul VI had given him and to all the Yugoslav bishops at the end of their common audience with him in the autumn of 1977. Mother Teresa accepted the gift with joy, and added "I am taking it, and if you have no objection, it will go to the first couple among our children who get married."

Through her houses, houses of love and schools of life, through her hands and those of her Sisters thousands of infants have passed. Today some of them have finished their studies, gotten married, and occupy responsible positions. Today they spread all over the world in various ways the capacity of loving and the respect which they learned from the Sisters.

The number of such houses is constantly growing, in India and in other places. Today the Missionaries of Charity successfully direct more than forty similar centers in India alone.

Struggle against leprosy

Leprosy has always been one of the most dangerous and widespread maladies in the world, not only on account of the illness itself, but also because of the neglect with which it has so often been treated. Leprosy is very prevalent in India, which counts over four million cases today. In the world as a whole there are over twenty million.

The problem of leprosy has absorbed many apostolic-minded people. Let us recall here the names of only two of these, who by their life and their work have drawn the interest and attention of the world to the agonizing problem of leprosy.

The pioneer was Fr. Damien de Veuster (1840-89), a Catholic priest who dedicated his entire life to the lepers in the Hawaiian islands. He lived among them for fourteen years, toiling day and night, and finally contracted the disease, from which he died.

The second was the founder of the International Federation against Leprosy, M. Raoul Follereau. He sought to rally all possible efforts to combat this plague, and also fought the neglect and inhumane treatment too often meted out to the victims of this disease.

On the fifteenth anniversary of the International Day of Struggle Against Leprosy (1961), M. Follereau wrote:

"If you can quietly sit and think, without remorse or emotion, that of the fifteen million lepers in the world (the disease is not really as contagious as you think) at least twelve million die without any medical care, attention or love, then you must be some kind of leper yourself."

In India, the Missionary Sisters of Charity take care of eighty hospitals specializing in the care of lepers. Mother Teresa came into contact with this burning question of our times while she was working among the poor. Her interest in the lepers was heightened by the decision made by the government of West Bengal and its head, Dr. Roya, to transfer from one area in Calcutta to another the ghetto of the lepers at Gobra, to a place farther out, as required by the city planning code. He and Mother Teresa were well acquainted and had often worked together, but on this point they did not see eye to eye. Their viewpoints were at variance. Mother Teresa wanted to go and see him and protest, but it was useless. Still it was precisely this initial failure that spurred her on to greater concern for the lepers.

The last straw was the case of five workingmen who, because of their leprosy had lost first their jobs and then their families. They had happened to come together, having nothing, and no one to turn to. All alone they were obliged to beg in the streets.

Mother Teresa wanted to help them, and all those who suffered like them. In this endeavor she was greatly aided by Dr. Senn, a specialist famous for dealing with leprosy. It was he who prepared the Sisters to carry out this difficult and dangerous task.

The Sisters' systematic service of the lepers began in 1957.

A few years ago Mother Teresa made the following statements:

"My Sisters, Brothers and I have charge of 46,000 lepers. We sold the fancy automobile that the Pope gave me during the Sixth Eucharistic Congress, and with this money we founded *Shanti Nagar* (City of Peace) for the lepers. In this locality alone we gathered together seven thousand of them. Every year we manage to cure over two hundred. Of course, everything is gratis."

Sister Bernarda relates:

"Some of the lepers are rich people. Some are university students with families in comfortable circumstances, well-known people, who come to us to get their medicine. I remember a girl who just before her marriage came to us in secret to get treatment. Her parents had noticed that on her body there had appeared the spots indicating leprosy, and they knew that the parents of her fiance would not have wanted him to marry her if they had discovered her condition. Fortunately, the girl got well.

"Leprosy deforms the victim, but these physical deformations are not what frighten them the most, but rather the idea of being expelled from their families and from society, of being shunned by all. As soon as the symptoms appear, the sick have to leave their families of their own accord; and the family wants to have nothing more to do with them. I think that this ostracism is far harder to bear than the malady itself. In fact there are some very contagious cases, but thank God these are rare. Even the patients who are not contagious are deformed; some have no hands, or eyes, or legs, so that people are afraid of them. In the rehabilitation centers they have every advantage: schools, hospitals, work places, stores to buy clothes and shoes, churches. . . . They can live an almost normal life."

I asked her how the lepers felt about the Sisters.

She answered:

"Let me tell you about an incident that happened. A very rich and distinguished man perceived that he had contracted leprosy. Right away he had to give up his family and his important job in the company. His wife had insisted on this: 'You know very well that if you do not leave the house our daughters will never be able to marry. So, go away.' He obeyed and sought asylum in a refuge for the poor. He asked for nothing, not even for medical attention; he just wanted to die in peace. One day our Sisters found him; they disinfected his sores and placed him in a bed. That day he changed, and said: 'Now I believe that God really loves me.'

"Today he is our best helper in all our undertakings, in assistance to the sick and in our school work. He has changed completely and was really born again when he realized that he was loved."

Leprosy and religious feeling among the Hindus

"Touch the leper with your goodness."

It was an extremely exhausting struggle, to do away with the Hindu notion that leprosy is a chastisement from God for the sins the sick person himself committed, or for those of his ancestors. In this perspective, any action against leprosy is an action contrary to the divine will. Such were the motives for the opposition she met with.

Mother Teresa relates: "It is very difficult to convince people in India that God never condemned people to suffer. We know of cases of stark tragedy in which people cured of leprosy were slain, sometimes by members of their own families. For this reason we resolved to build little villages for them, where they could live, work, and eventually have a family. Today leprosy can be treated successfully; obviously if it is caught in time. It takes about six months. Thanks to our benefactors the work is proceeding well, and many people have recovered the will to live."

Because of the widespread prejudice against them, most of the lepers flee into the mountains, where they go about from place to place, begging and living in isolation, like animals. They avoid the healthy for fear of infecting them, and they flee the police too, who throw them into detention camps, where they have neither help nor care, and soon die.

But now, after so many sacrifices made by Mother Teresa and others, people are beginning to understand that leprosy is an illness, nothing else.

When she protested to the Bengalese government which wanted to transfer the lepers from Gobra to another location in Calcutta, she did not succeed in making the authorities change their decision, but she did manage to delay the move until adequate installations had been made available. The first location had not satisfied her, and she complained to the president: "You had told me that you would give me a decent location. The place you now offer me lacks water, which for the lepers is something absolutely indispensable."

It then occurred to her to organize a "leper collection day." So she went about the whole city with little jars on which was written: "Touch the lepers with your goodness." Money began to flow in from all sides. The people displayed full understanding of what she needed.

From this collection and from other gifts was born the *Shanti Nager* (City of Peace), a center for health care and a place for the sick lepers and those who have been cured, from the region of Burdwan. It is run by Dr. Sister Francis Xavier Orzes, a qualified physician.

While engaged in this trail-breaking and heroic task, Sister Francis and some other Sisters contracted leprosy. They refused any special care or special place for cure, and remained among the lepers like all the rest.

Mother Teresa says: "There are thousands and millions of lepers in the world. One Christmas I went to visit them, and told them that God loved them very specially; that all they had was God's gift; that God was close to them; that their illness was no sin. An old man, hardly able to move, with difficulty came up to me and said: 'Please, repeat that once more; I never before heard anything of the kind. All my life I only heard that nobody wanted me. How beautiful it is to know that God loves me!' "

Where others see only pain and darkest misery, Christians should proclaim Christ who is suffering.

Mother Teresa thus explained her way of looking at it all: "When I touch those foul-smelling limbs I know that I am touching the body of Christ, just as under the appearance of bread I receive him in communion. This conviction gives me strength and courage. I surely could not do what I do if I did not believe that in the wasted limbs of the lepers I am touching Jesus."

Struggle against abortion

"Abortion is the beginning of evil in the world" (Mother Teresa at Oslo, 1979).

Mother Teresa, living a life like that of the poor, soon came to realize that their great misfortune was not poverty; there were others. Therefore, as we have stated, she began to undertake the building of hospitals, of homes for the aged, for abandoned babies, for the lepers, and so on.

Today she openly wars against abortion and for the infant's right to live. She speaks in the name of those who cannot speak for themselves. Openly to the world she affirms that abortion is the plague of our time, a constant threat to the whole human race.

This is what she said at Catania in 1977: "In the last twenty-seven years dedicated to the poor we have helped thousands of needy people, and we have never turned anyone away since we always had something to give. Here is an example: A certain person got sick; she needed some medicine unobtainable in India. I was in a position to get this medicine anywhere I asked for it and wanted it. I was about to send someone to go and get it when a man came in, bringing a packet of medicines. We opened it, and on the top of the package there was precisely the product we needed so badly."

At the grandiose celebration for life on April 23, at Milan, Italy, Mother Teresa spoke at the San Siro Stadium in the presence of 100,000 persons; she discussed the problem of abortion, spoke of human dignity and the right to life.

"The life of the unborn child is a gift of God, the greatest gift God can make to the family. Today there are many countries which permit abortion, sterilization and other means for avoiding or destroying life, from its very inception. This is a clear sign that such countries are the poorest among the poor, since they do not have the courage to accept even one more life.

"The life of a baby not yet born, like the life of the poor that we find in the streets of Calcutta and other parts of the world, the life of children and that of adults, is still the same life. It is our life. It is a gift from God.

"I am not discussing whether there is any need to legalize abortion or not. I simply believe that no human hand has the right to cut down a life. Every existence is the life of God in us; even the unborn child has divine life in itself. We have no right to annihilate that life, by whatever means. Man, woman, child . . . it makes no difference. It seems to me that the cry of the unborn rises up to us: those children slaughtered before they even came into the world; an accusation which reechoes before God's throne."

She spoke boldly on this subject before a worldwide audience which was following the ceremony of the awarding of the Nobel Peace Prize, in December, 1979.

Chapter 5
Life with God

Prayer

To carry out such a task, strength is needed, and unlimited courage. Mother Teresa always stresses that her work and that of her Sisters is the work of God, that its origin and effectiveness come from God himself. For this reason prayer is an element of major importance in their lives.

"All the work carried on by our Sisters, all that we do, is nothing but the fruit of prayer, of our union with Jesus in the holy eucharist, especially holy communion. Thanks to this we can every day work very much, with a large number of lepers, the dying, the little ones, and others. Every evening when we come home we make an hour of adoration. This is the biggest treasure of the community of the Missionaries of Charity. From this we draw our strength.

"We frequent the houses of the poor and the streets where people are dying of hunger. The convent is necessary for us only for a couple of hours of rest and prayer. Our life, without the strength which we derive from prayer, would be impossible."

Prayer, meditation, adoration of the Most Blessed Sacrament, are the daily food of the Missionaries of Charity. This is certainly the secret of their success on a worldwide scale.

Prayer played an important role in Mother Teresa's life and in her spiritual growth. From her youth at home, she learned how to speak with God. During her maturing years, from twelve to eighteen, she sought in prayer the answer to her search for the God's will. Even today she willingly remembers those marvelous times, full of good fortune and of happiness for her and for the whole Bojaxhiu family.

"When I remember my mother, my father and the others, praying together every evening . . . I hope that our Albanian families have remained faithful to this custom, for this is the greatest gift God can give them to maintain union in families. The family that does not pray together cannot live united. So, go back to family prayer, and keep to it. By means of prayer you will discover your own mission" (to the faithful of Albania, at Zagreb, June 10, 1970).

Although her Sisters were laboring day and night, with scarcely any rest, still every item had its proper place among them, and its own time, especially prayer. The Sisters prayed walking through the streets, when going to work or coming home. They knew that without prayer they would not persevere for long.

Regarding the spirit of her Company she once said:

"In the world we are a contemplative religious society. When there are no more poor people, starving people or lepers, we will come back to our convents to dedicate ourselves entirely to sacrifice and prayer."

As she said this she stopped a moment, her face wearing a special smile filled with angelic peace. She opened her arms, looked up to heaven, and continued: "But I think that time will never come. It would seem that we have little competition in our type of work. Suffering and poverty are found everywhere. And it is not only material poverty I speak of, for spiritual suffering and misery are constantly growing."

One day I went to see her with a colleague of mine who was eager to be introduced to her. The conversation began at once: few words, but well chosen and weighty, and full of faith. Mother gazed at him for a long time and then, on a holy picture, she wrote: "You are called to holiness, to God's complete service, to guide God's people towards the light. So that you may obtain this for yourself and for your faithful, pray much with a pure heart and with great faith. Abandon yourself entirely to God's guidance. Do not hesitate or be frightened. God bless you." Mother Teresa.

My colleague and confrere remained speechless. Almost stammering, and deeply moved, he told me later:

"Until this day no one has ever understood me better, or touched me to the quick as Mother Teresa did. She put her finger on my problem."

Still later he avowed to me that he was undergoing a difficult and painful situation.

In March, 1974, Mother Teresa wrote to the Sisters about prayer: "We have only one prayer, one specific, fundamental prayer: this is Jesus Christ himself. Only one voice rises from earth to heaven, the voice of Jesus Christ. . . . Hence, prayer means first of all being united with Christ. Many vocations are facing a crisis; many will not come to maturity; many families experience difficulties, are falling apart and are being dissolved; a lot of people have lost all taste for life and for work; they are discontented and empty solely because they have given up and forgotten prayer.

"I keep coming back to the capital point: keep silent. Silence and love. Speaking little, keeping silence and peace make us able to hear the voice of Christ. Keeping silent (like closing our eyes) enables us to see God. Our two eyes are two windows through which both Christ and the world come in. Very often we must be brave and strong in spirit to keep our eyes shut.

"Work without love is slavery. Of us the Church expects renewal. Renewal does not signify changing laws, rules, prayers; it means above all being faithful to God and to the rules, or better, to the spirit of our religious rule."

Mass and communion

Holy Mass and daily communion, divine food and personal encounter with Christ, are for the Sisters the most important moments of the day, says Mother Teresa. Armed with Christ and God the Sisters go out to work among the poor and the lepers, in a world filled with the deepest misery.

She continued: "As Jesus Christ became bread, food for us, He is at our disposal for our life; and thus He is our life; so too should we be for others, for every human being. We must become bread for the others."

Thus, the source of the divine power to dedicate oneself to others is the daily encounter with God, especially through holy communion. On December 5, 1975, she wrote to her brother Lazzaro in Italy the following notes on divine love and on holy communion. "He is infinite love. He alone can fill your life. He alone can truly love you. He alone is happiness and peace for our hearts. Our good Jesus remains in the tabernacle for me and for you, so that you and I can receive him in our hearts every day. My brother, go to Jesus; He will fill your soul with joy, love and immense peace that the whole world can neither give you nor take away. Pray for me; as I pray for you.

"Mass is the spiritual food that nourishes me. Without it I could not survive for a day or an hour in the life I lead. Jesus comes to us in the Mass under the appearance of bread. In the slums of the city we touch Jesus in pain-racked bodies and abandoned babies."

We see clearly how Mother Teresa grasps the identification with Christ in every human being, especially in the least. Her desire and her command is to do good to all, without any distinction, as though it was being done by God himself.

After a eucharistic adoration she said:

"Now we are leaving the chapel to know, love and serve the same Jesus whom we adored in the holy eucharist. You see, we are happy because we can remain in contact with Jesus twenty-four hours a day."

And again:

"For love to be true it does not need to be special; special things are not needed; they must simply be addressed to Christ whom we love. How does a lamp burn? Always, continually, and slowly. The oil burns drop by drop. When there is no more oil the flame stops burning and there is no more light. My dearest Sisters, what are, in our lives, in our hearts, in our labors those tiny drops in the lamp? They are the little things of every day: by faithfulness and exactness they show love. So, do not seek Jesus outside of your life, but rather within yourselves, in your hearts, in holy communion. After that you can seek, find and serve him in others. Keep your lamps burning, and you will constantly find him."

To help them understand this idea as clearly as possible Mother Teresa often cited the action of Our Lady when she had made her "first communion" in other words when she knew she was going to become the mother of God, when she had the Son of God incarnate within her. Mary immediately set out to visit her cousin Elizabeth, to help her and serve her, but especially to bring Christ to her. The same thing should happen in communion. Nourished with Christ's body the Sister must live and work with and for others, convinced that her true mission is to bring Christ with her. Hence, holy communion is not just a passive thing; we don't receive it just for ourselves; nor is it a purely private matter, but an action that spurs us on to action, to a life of dedication, with strength, energy and conscience, especially by our active presence and testimony.

"The fruit of our union with Jesus is the vow of love, like the child is the fruit of the sacrament of matrimony. The lamp does not burn without oil, nor can the vow of love exist without the vows of poverty and obedience."

Once, when I was a university student in Rome I went with several companions to visit the Sisters' house in a poor section of the city. It was a Thursday, the day dedicated solely to prayer, meditation and adoration. After a few words we went into the chapel together with Mother Teresa for adoration. We knelt with her, and remained there for several hours. She was as immobile as a statue, wrapped in contemplation. We remained there for four hours; I was getting tired and bored, so I was very glad when the time of adoration ended. As we left the chapel I asked: "Mother, didn't you get tired? Weren't you bored?"

She was very serene, and her face and aspect were those of an angel as she said: "No. How could I get tired or bored when I am with God, in his company, in the presence of his love? For me, the difficult thing is to tear myself away; but now I must continue praying in another way. Now we must go and recognize in our neighbors the same Christ whom we were beholding under the species of bread."

She noticed that I was tired, because I was moving to the right and to the left as if trying to read something; then she said to me, almost casually: "Ask God to give you his love too, as He has given it to me. This is a gift of his. Pray, and he will certainly give it to you because he is rich, and has gifts for all."

Devotion to the Mother of God

Teresa's fervent devotion to Our Lady was deeply rooted, going back to her earliest childhood. When she was still very young she used to say the rosary in the family. At fifteen she joined the Sodality of Our Lady.

"Every evening we gathered around our mother (whom she called 'Loke,' the endearing term used by the Albanians for their grandmothers) since Daddy was often away. Generally, we said the rosary."

Even today Mother Teresa does not forget Our Lady of Letnice and the old Albanian hymn "On the black mountain (of Skopje) we have our mother." She still sings it with childlike enthusiasm and with tears in her eyes.

"It was at Letnice that for the first time I heard God's voice; my vocation convinced me that I should serve God and be at his disposal. I remember the feast of Mary's Assumption, when before Mary's altar, and with a burning candle in my hand, and singing with my heart about to burst, I had decided: 'I want to belong to God!'"

In 1970 when she came back to her country for the first time in forty-two years, she visited her home town of Skopje and went to Letnice. With deep devotion and immense joy she stopped to pray for a long time before the Madonna. Then she got up and looked fixedly at the statue of the mother of her mission saying, "They have changed her dress; it is not the same one she wore long ago. But her eyes and her face are still the same."

At Oslo too she spoke with nostalgia of Letnice and of Our Lady.

"Do all you can so that I may see Skopje again, and open the first house in August for the feast of Our Lady of Letnice. Today I remember that it was there, precisely, that I first felt my call. There I decided to consecrate myself to God and to my neighbor. At the time, of course, I kept this all to myself. I remember so well those beautiful days, especially the hymn. I want to go back there to thank her for everything."

In her letters one can observe how deeply she was bound to Our Lady of Letnice. Writing to her brother Lazzaro's family

(May 5, 1974) she recommends herself to their prayers.

When she established her first religious community, the Missionaries of Charity, she dedicated it to Our Lady and decided that its patronal feast would be August 22, the feast of the Immaculate Heart of Mary.

In the rules of the Missionaries of Charity, Mary is called "our protectress" and in several places devotion towards her is stressed.

Let us cite some reflections, taken from the letters which from time to time she wrote to the Sisters.

"My dear Sisters: October 7 is for us a day of thanksgiving, since our community was born on that day. For this reason it belongs to the Mother of God alone. It is a great favor to march ahead under her protection. It is our duty to develop like a tree, straight and tall, and covered with fruit."

Our Lady is the model for the Sisters' religious life.

They should follow her footsteps in the path of virtue. "Let us pray to Our Lady, our mother, to grant us the grace to be, with all our hearts, humble and obedient like the heart of her Son. We are called to great things; why, therefore, should we tarry behind in what is mean and empty?

"The greatness of Our Lady and our own, resides in humility. Humility is very necessary in our life, because we are in this world along with other human beings. People love us and are grateful to us for what we do, but we must always remain humble, because our work is really God's work."

Mother Teresa and her family

Mother Teresa always remembers her family with deep love. This is not just a sentimental throwback to her childhood and youth, but a close bond uniting her with her origins.

Of course, at Skopje, things are very different now from what they were formerly.

Her mother played a decisive role in her early youth, like a real flame of fire, inspiring the whole family. Often, in interviews, she stresses how important a mother's role is in the family.

"Once, in London, I met a young Hippie busily destroying himself with alcohol and drugs. I stopped him and said: 'You are so young; you should not be out on the street all the time.' He told me: 'My mother does not love me because I have long hair; I don't know where else to go, so I am staying here.'

"An hour later I passed by the same spot, but he was gone. Someone told me that he was an addict and had been taken to a hospital, in danger of death. Perhaps he was already dead."

She told me of another typical example.

"A twenty-one-year-old girl in despair wanted to commit suicide because her mother, that morning, had scolded her severely. In the hospital, after they had saved her she told a priest: 'My mother threw me out of the house. I didn't know what to do. So I decided that the best thing was to commit suicide.' Families are responsible for much of the suffering of the young, mothers especially. We must be like mothers for our communities, so that they may become happy, resplendent places."

In Oslo, on the day she received the Nobel Peace Prize, when asked "What is the greatest threat to peace today?" she answered: "Today, the biggest threat to peace is abortion, killing unborn children. In fact, if we have a right to suppress the life that has been given by God, if a mother can put her own child to death, then how can we condemn all the other assassins in the world? This is why murder is getting more and more common."

Although so taken up with so many activities, Mother Teresa always managed to think of her family; and when it was possible she wrote to her mother, Drana, to her sister Aga in Albania, and to her brother in Italy.

She longed to see them all once more in this life. In 1960 she visited her brother Lazzaro and his wife Maria, their daughter Aga and her husband Joseph.

Their meeting in Rome was truly moving. It was the first since 1924. On this occasion Lazzaro mentioned that they should do something to see once again their mother and sister, who were still in Albania. He told her, as he said to me, "Dear Agnes, don't lose hope; now we have many friends all over the world. I hope I will be able to do something for them."

Lazzaro showed me the letters from Drana and Aga, sent from the capital of Albania, Tirana. They were filled with nostalgia, and with the yearning to see Agnes and himself. For instance:

"How happy your few lines made me! It is as though I had seen you again. You don't know, my dearest, how much I love you, and how I long to see you again, as soon as possible. The same goes for our dearest Mamma, who always keeps your photo on her breast. I still do not see any way of going to embrace you, and to rejoice with you, but maybe the time will come. You know how this loneliness afflicts me. Just the thought of having you close again makes me happy, and perhaps some day I shall see you. So, please, write.

"From Agnes I have not heard for a long time. Of course she has much to do, and little time to spend with me. I am grateful to her because she promised to come and visit me when I can visit you. I am glad she is well. Today I will write to her too. A big hug, and lots of kisses. Your sister, Aga."

In 1962, Msgr. Branko Dorcic from Ohrid, first succeeded in making contact by letter with Mother Teresa. He also wrote to three other religious, who were also in the mission along with Mother Teresa: these were Sister Gabriella, born at Skopje, and who went to the missions following the footsteps of Agnes, in 1931. She remained with the Lorettine Sisters until her death which occurred in India in 1974. Sister Magdalena, Betika Kajnc, a Slovene girl who made the journey with Agnes to Ireland and India, as we have already mentioned; and Sister Frances Xavier, Giuseppina Orzes, the daughter of immigrants from Banja Luka, originally from Istria, who settled in Skopje. At first she had joined the Lorettines with the name of Sister Bernarda; then in 1951 she joined the Missionaries of Charity with the name of Sister Frances Xavier. She got a doctorate in medicine, caught leprosy, but was cured of it. Today she is in charge of the City of Peace. In his letter Msgr. Dorcic informed her of the situation in his diocese, and mentioned the many new vocations, the renovation of the church of the Sacred Heart of Jesus at Skopje, which had been threatened by the flood waters from the river Vardar. All this was before the catastrophic earthquake in the summer of 1963, which destroyed the church.

He got a reply from Mother Teresa, in which, among other things, she said:

"Dear and reverend Father: Your letter brought me news of Skopje after thirty-three years! You can imagine my joy in reading it. I thank you. God has blessed Skopje. I think that our poor people who suffer so much are praying for you and for Skopje. I am so glad to hear that there are so many vocations. . . . Here, our Company is growing steadily. We now have 149 Sisters. Pray for the new houses we have opened. Ever since I have been in India nobody has ever invited me to Blagovest; I suppose that people in Skopje have completely forgotten Agnes. You are the first one who wrote to me. Pray for me, and I too pray for our people in Skopje, hoping that they will pray for me too. My mother and my sisters are still in Tirana. God alone knows why they must suffer so much. Surely their sacrifices and prayers help me in my task. All for the greater glory of God! In June, it will be a great day for our church in Skopje, the church of the Sacred Heart of Jesus. In that little church I received the first inklings of my vocation. Pray for me and I shall do the same for you."

In a letter dated January 4, 1970, Aga wrote about their mother, Drana: "Mother is weakening so much that sometimes she does not even recognize me. She is very thin and weighs only ninety pounds. I am all right, but everything is very difficult. Mamma and Aga."

On December 4, 1971 she wrote again: "Dear ones: we are about the same; Mother is weak from her illness. I would so love to be close to you to help you and be happy together. On New Year's eve I shall be close to you in thought and heart, just as I am sure you two think of mother and Aga.

"I did not hear from Agnes. It seems she does not remember us any more, with all she has to do. When you write to her greet her in my name too. Mamma and Aga."

Lazzaro showed me many letters from Drana and Aga, and also from Mother Teresa in Calcutta. Here is one of the most touching.

Drana writes:

"My only wish is to see you once more before I die, your family and my beloved Agnes."

Considering the difficult and painful situation affecting her scattered family, Mother Teresa tried to see them one last time. Once she went to the Albanian embassy in Rome together with another Sister and Ms. Eileen Egan, the Indian inspectress of the Catholic Relief Services of the U.S. Catholic Conference. This lady was an old friend of Mother Teresa, and in Oslo she told us this:

"They did not even want to speak with her. When Mother Teresa left the embassy I saw her, for the first time, with tears in her eyes. She stopped, raised her eyes to heaven and said: 'O God, I understand and accept my own suffering, but it is difficult for me to understand my mother's and to accept it, because in her old age all she desires is to see us once more.' "

Although she had failed at the embassy, she did not give up. It seemed that various personalities of worldwide importance such as President John F. Kennedy, General Charles de Gaulle, U Thant, Indira Gandhi and others tried to help her; but it was all in vain.

Lazzaro tells us: "One day Teresa told me: 'Up to now I have succeeded in obtaining everything with love and prayer; but there are still barriers and obstacles that even love does not succeed in breaking down.' "

The very day when Mother Teresa in Rome was trying to get into the Albanian embassy, and when she uttered her heartfelt prayer for her old mother, Drana was writing to her, through Aga, for the last time. The letter read: "Even if we don't see each other again on this wretched earth, we shall certainly see each other in heaven."

On July 12, 1972, Lazzaro Bojaxhiu received this telegram:

"Today, July 12, at five o'clock, Mother died. Aga (Tirana #282)."

For him and for his whole family it was a crushing blow. He wired Teresa: "Mother Teresa Bojaxhiu: 54 A Lower, Calcutta, India. Pray for Mother who died on July 12. Lazzaro. Palermo, July 14, 1972." No sooner had she received the telegram than she went to the chapel and prayed for a long time.

For Aga it was more difficult than for the others because she had to remain in Albania completely alone, with no one near her. She had been living close to her mother Drana ever since she had become a young widow. In a letter dated July 27, 1973, she wrote to Lazzaro: "My dear ones, I am often bored, ever since I am without our dear Mother. Ah, how I miss her; but she is gone and will not return. I hope that I may be able to come to you, and then everything will be so much easier. I have not heard from Agnes, as though she had already begun to forget her sister. When you write, remember me to her. Aga."

Neither did this hope ever find realization for Aga Bojaxhiu. She died without ever having seen either her sister or Lazzaro again.

Theirs was truly a tormented family, separated in life in every way. From a purely human point of view, theirs was a cruel destiny.

Resemblances between Drana Bojaxhiu and Mother Teresa

Drana Bojaxhiu (Loke, as her children called her), in her early years and at the start of her married life was a calm and satisfied person. She lived harmoniously in a house filled with love. This period of her life was probably the preparation for the trials which would come to her later.

The first of these was the death of her husband, Kole Bojaxhiu, who died of internal bleeding, but under suspicious circumstances.

The second was the departure of her only son, Lazzaro, who went to study abroad; and then, even more difficult for her to bear, the departure of her youngest daughter for the convent.

The third and perhaps the most difficult was the transfer to Albania where she remained entirely separated from her son and her youngest daughter, and where in her old age she lived with but a single desire in her heart: to see Agnes and Lazzaro one last time before dying. But this desire was never fulfilled. She died in sorrow and solitude; her only company Aga and God.

Those who know her well claim that Mother Teresa took after her mother a great deal. They also resemble each other in the destiny that befell them. Like her mother, Mother Teresa enjoyed a peaceful youth. Her first test, her first separation was her vocation to go far away, to India, to serve God and her neighbor. There she was a teacher for nearly twenty years. She herself says that this was a time when she tasted great satisfaction in her work, but it did not make her happy.

God called her to take care of the poorest of the poor. She had to begin all over again from scratch. This second mission was her second trial.

The third cross was in the difficulties we mentioned in trying to see her mother again, at least once before the latter died. But in this world that trial was not to be overcome.

Chapter 6
Growth of Missionary Love

"You will be my witnesses . . . to the ends of the earth" (Acts 1:8).

After the founding of the Company of the Missionaries of Charity, days went by, and months, and years. The number of vocations increased. With this the work increased too, but also the dedication and the opportunities.

Ten years of activity spelled progress in vocations and in the missions.

The life of the community was at first restricted mostly to Calcutta and its environs. Slowly the conditions needed came into being, so that the community might spread outside of Calcutta. This period, which Mother Teresa calls the third phase of her life, followed from the first and the second. Circumstances were favorable for this, for vocations came in from various parts of India. The Sisters were more mature and grew accustomed to the new lifestyle. There was of course no slackening in the needs. A specially clear proof of this was given by the requests from various bishops, who wished to have the Missionaries of Charity in their dioceses.

Mother Teresa reflected carefully about this stage of the operation. It could be very useful and fruitful; but it could also prove dangerous, for the Sisters would be dispersed, and thus the community might disintegrate. But, as we have already mentioned, she finally decided to make a start.

Expansion in India

Mother Teresa's Sisters first went to Ranchi, in the mission of Ghota Nagpur, which had formerly been part of the archdiocese of Calcutta. Today this new diocese is the hope of the Catholic Church in northern India. From it there have already arisen many vocations, and there are even more now. The first house outside of Calcutta was opened on May 26, 1959. Besides the diocese of Ranchi, others sorely needed the Sisters.

Archbishop Joseph Fernandes of Delhi had for some time been asking Mother Teresa for Sisters; he had been vicar general and auxiliary bishop of Calcutta. Although it was a most important center, and the capital, Delhi had very few Catholics. Through Mother Teresa the archbishop wished to display the Catholic religion, and Christ himself, in a convincing manner.

This occasion too was providential; it brought the Missionaries of Charity closer to the capital of India. It is the most beautiful and the largest city in India, but its suburbs are very poor, for thousands of people have come in from the countryside, and often spend their lives in the most appalling misery, without shelter or any social help. The Swiss ambassador, Mr. Cuttat, a deeply convinced and practicing Catholic, did a great deal to insure the opening of a hospice for babies in Delhi.

At the ceremony of the inauguration of the first house, in June 1959, the president of India, Jawaharlal Nehru and several members of his government were present. This was the start of the good relationships between Mother Teresa and the Indian government. Nehru met her several times, and got to know her personally. When she attempted to explain to him the activity of her Missionaries he broke in: "I know about your work; that is why I have come here today."

The third house outside of Calcutta was opened in 1960 at Jansi. At first the Sisters worked mostly with poor children and orphans, and opened schools for them. Then, day after day their activity expanded to other fields: caring for the needy, the lepers, the sick and the aged.

At the same time houses were opened at Agra, Asansol, Amhala (all in 1961), then at Amravat, Bhagelpur and Bombay, in 1962. The number of houses was growing with unexpected success. No one had foreseen such rapid growth. We shall mention only the most important fou idations.

Bombay is one of the leading metropolises of India, at least with regard to culture, finance and commerce. The Catholic community is relatively large and well organized. For this reason, and for others as well, Mother Teresa wanted to have a house in Bombay too. At the time the local archbishop was the first Indian cardinal, Valerian Gracias. Mother Teresa wrote to him. The meeting was fruitful. The Cardinal already knew of her and her work. They quickly came to an agreement for he too was anxious to have the Sisters in Bombay.

In this case, too, as in that of all the new houses, Mother Teresa personally concerned herself; she wanted to see the premises, to verify the requirements and conditions, so that the Sisters might prepare themselves as well as possible for their new mission. For this reason she went about the whole city on foot, from one end to the other, and remained amazed by the frightful poverty she saw, and the way the people were neglected and left to their own resources.

She once said: "It seems to me that in Bombay there are more poor people than in Calcutta. The housing available to them is a sheer disgrace."

Such a statement did not at first endear her to many people, especially the rich. They were offended by the unfavorable comparison with Calcutta, which was notorious for its filth, its poor, its lepers, and for everything evil, whereas Bombay was considered the richest city in India, a center of social and cultural life. Some newspapers openly criticized Mother Teresa for her remarks; no one could speak that way about Bombay! Nobody, especially a stranger, could say things like that, so inaccurate and unfavorable! But after a few hours spent in the metropolis she knew the facts better than the citizens themselves.

A parish priest offered her a large house. She found it possible to make use of the place; and in 1962 she opened the first refuge for abandoned children.

Many people saw in this a faint ray of hope, especially the Catholic priests with the Cardinal at their head; but even more so did the ordinary people and the needy. After a while even the newspapers which had criticized her were forced to admit: "Now in Bombay nobody dies all alone in the streets. Mother Teresa, a woman small in stature, but great in spirit, day and night battles, with her Sisters, against death, leprosy, and poverty. This is a divine gift for us."

At first the Missionaries of Charity had ten Sisters in Bombay. A year later, when the Eucharistic Congress took place (November 29, 1964), Mother Teresa started out to attend the inaugural ceremony, but never arrived. On the street leading to the palace where the Congress was to take place, she met two dying people near a tree, a man and his wife. With their last remaining strength they moved along, helping one another. They were nothing but skin and bones, and their faces were bloody. Without losing a moment Mother Teresa came up to them and took them by the hand. After a few words, the man died in her arms. She picked up his wife on her shoulders and brought her to the house of the dying. She did not get to the opening ceremony of the Congress, nor did she see the pope that day.

During his visit Pope Paul VI expressed the desire of visiting the poor quarters of Bombay. He remained deeply moved by the work undertaken by Mother Teresa, and made up his mind to do something about it.

"Before I leave our beloved India," he said, "I wish to donate this white motorcar to Mother Teresa, the superior general of the Missionaries of Charity, to help her in her great work of love."

As we mentioned earlier, this car, a Lincoln, helped Mother Teresa to open, at the beginning of 1969 the *Shanti Nagar* (City of Peace), the first big hospital and center for the treatment of leprosy. The automobile had been given to the pope by a wealthy American.

Gradually, other houses were opened in various places in India: Patna (1963), Paringas, Jamshedpur, Old Goa, Darjeeling (1964) and so on. Today the Missionaries of Charity are established in practically all the dioceses of India.

In South America

The success achieved by the Sisters and their increasing number, the new vocations which kept coming from all parts of the world, along with the requests of numerous bishops, led Mother Teresa to take into consideration new proposals, and to consider new possibilities.

Among the first invitations was one from a Venezuelan bishop, Msgr. Benitez. After taking the advice of her counsellors and of the spiritual father, Mother Teresa decided to send some of her best religious there. Thus, in 1965, the first house in Venezuela was opened, at Cocorota near Caracas, a small city with many poor people in it. The first superioress was Sister Dorothy; other Sisters had many qualifications: doctors, counsellors, teachers. Most of the people in Venezuela had been baptized, but knew little about their religion; they had hardly heard Jesus Christ spoken of. The Sisters also worked as catechists and pastoral helpers; when it was necessary they administered baptism, visited the sick, and sometimes distributed holy communion.

Sister Dorothy comments: "This was something new for us, a remarkable experience, something never before attempted. How necessary we are to God, especially in Latin America, to bring him to the people."

Another Sister relates: "In Venezuela we are almost priests! We do just about everything except hear confessions and say Mass. The task here is marvelous."

In 1970 two other houses were opened in Venezuela, and in 1973 another at Lima, Peru. Later on, Mother Teresa was asked to come to Colombia, Bolivia and Brazil. However, in Latin America things did not always turn out as well as expected. The Church authorities wanted the Sisters to undertake more social and pastoral activity in the parishes, whereas the Missionaries wished to be especially of service to the poor. Although they had soon learned Spanish, and had rapidly won the affection of the people, vocations were few and far between. Besides, there were many obstacles to be overcome, arising from the social and political situation. This encounter with the complex realities in South America, with the local church and with the people, was of great advantage to the Company.

Once Mother Teresa spoke thus of Latin America: "What a vast field is open there to the apostolate. There is so much poverty, misery, ignorance, and yet such hunger and thirst for spiritual goods."

At Rome

In March 1968, Pope Paul VI invited Mother Teresa by a personal letter to come and open a house in Rome. In this letter the Pope enclosed a round trip airplane ticket, Calcutta-Rome, and a check for ten thousand dollars. Mother Teresa was very happy over this invitation.

On August 22, 1968, she left for Rome accompanied by Sister Federica. She told us about this occasion:

"When the pope called on me I could not refuse. During our conversation I told him: 'I am ready to open a house, if there are poor people to be served.' "

Once she had visited the city and had seen the wretched social and economic conditions that existed in the outskirts, she came back to the pope and told him: "Your Holiness, God seems to have left work for us to do, just about everywhere."

In Rome she opened not only that first house, but also a novitiate and a refuge for alcoholics, for the aged, and for the street people.

When I was a student in Rome I went with a few companions to visit the house and to greet Mother Teresa. It was rather difficult to find the house, in the streets which went nowhere, in the slum areas of the city. Nothing distinguished it very much from the surrounding shacks made mostly of old planks.

We inquired of some people passing by, but without much success. Finally, after having wandered about aimlessly we decided to inquire at some church. In one of these we found a priest, a teacher in a high school, and asked him where we could find Mother Teresa and her Sisters. He thought for a moment, and then told us, ironically: "Oh, yes! You are looking for those Indian Sisters who go about hunting for the gypsies, live with them, and bring disgrace to the Church!"

This reply shocked us, but since he had given us the information we needed we finally succeeded in locating the house of the "Indian Sisters," as people called them. It was a small, very poor house, like so many others around it. Fortunately, we found Mother Teresa there. This was not my first meeting with her. She welcomed us kindly and cordially. We spoke of her work in India with the poor and the lepers, and also of our home dioceses of Skopje and Prizren. I was amazed by the simplicity and the attention with which she listened to me. I found her a deeply thoughtful woman, with tiny body and hands, full of enthusiasm, a woman of deep convictions and burning love. When one was with her one had the impression of being outside of time and space; one felt tranquil, secure and happy, like a child close to its mother. So full of joy were we that we could not believe our good fortune. Together with her we sang "At Letnice we have a Mother"; then we went out to visit the neighborhood.

What was there to see? Nothing but the profoundest want. How often had I not passed by these shacks without ever noticing their sorry condition. There, not far away, the road leading to the Roman Castelli seemed to separate two different worlds. On one side the elegant, modern city, with its magnificent buildings (apparently magnificent, anyway), while on the other side huts made of old planks, corrugated iron or cardboard marred the landscape. Some families had caused some damage to the aqueduct (one of the ancient Roman aqueducts) today called the *aqua felix*; and there, between the arches they had set up housekeeping, without either water, electricity or heat, without doors or windows. What misery and degradation! I could not imagine that anything like this could exist in Rome, that majestic world metropolis.

Not far away there were acres of junked cars. People called this place the "auto graveyard": a monument to modern consumerism, to unlimited waste, existing side by side with people who were struggling to survive, and who longed only for a crust of bread. That visit opened our eyes to Roman reality, and to "how the other half lived."

From that day onward Mother Teresa became, in a way, a part of our life. Her house in Rome was an oasis in our spiritual life and in our vocation. That part of the city became dear to us, and so did the poor and their families, and the children of the neighborhood. To this day I can never forget them.

Right away I wrote down my impressions about meeting Mother Teresa. Here are some extracts:

"I cannot understand the simplicity, the love and the dedication Mother Teresa shows to the poor, nor can I grasp the peace of soul, the attention and the love she shared with us. She is a nun different from the rest. Different too is her lifestyle and that of her Sisters. How far we are from the gospel, while she is putting it into practice day by day as she lives among these people."

So that the Missionaries of Charity might be even more present in the Eternal City and that the Sisters might deepen their interior life even more, she transferred the novitiate from London to Rome.

The Sisters opened another special house in the center of the city, not far from the Termini railroad station. There they gathered together the alcoholics, the aged, the drug addicts, the homeless and the abandoned. At night they are helped by students belonging to various Catholic organizations.

After she was awarded the Nobel Peace Prize, Mother Teresa was received in audience by Pope John Paul II, who asked her to open a house for unmarried mothers; their number is ever on the increase, and they meet with ever increasing difficulties.

Besides their foundation in Rome the Sisters opened another house at Ostia, near Rome (1973), at Palermo in Sicily (1974) where her brother Lazzaro lives, then at Naples (1975), at Ragusa (Sicily), and at Reggio Calabria (1979).

Not long ago I visited the Sisters at Palermo. The poor section is right in the center of the old city. Next to the crumbling buildings I found the convent, where six Missionaries live today. This convent has become a new oasis of love and of Christian witness. There the Sisters take care of forty old people, abandoned without anyone to love or care for them.

During our conversation one of the old men told me: "This old quarter of poor people isn't poor any longer. For us it has become a corner of the earthly paradise. My own children abandoned me; they say they have their own careers (one is a doctor), but neither God nor these Sisters abandoned me."

The Sisters had opened this house in 1974. Mother Teresa chose this particular section of the city at the request of Cardinal Pappalardo. The Sisters relate that "when Mother Teresa visited the city and had seen it all, she said to the Cardinal: 'this quarter is just right for us.' "

When faced with certain repulsive sights, one instinctively draws back, and begins to wonder whether one can really help. I asked the Sisters how they felt when they found themselves here. They told me:

"At first it was rather difficult. People here live in isolation; they hardly see any reason to keep on living at all. Obviously, they have only the haziest ideas about God. With our witness and our affection we woke them from their torpor, and gave them something to think about in connection with human values. By now both they and we have grasped that many things can be changed. The improvement is obvious. Our little children are very easily distinguished from the rest. There is still much to be done among them, with the young people, with the families, and on the parish level. But even in the long range programs things have begun to move. Let us hope. . . ."

Later, the superioress told me about this dramatic story: "For four years this old man had lived and slept on the street. We offered to take him in, but he always refused. He finally gave in when we told him that ruffians might assault him, or the police arrest him. At first he told us he was not married and had no relatives. After about a year a lady arrived from Florence, saying that she was his daughter. We let him know about this, and he was amazed; then between sobs he confessed: 'Forgive me for not telling you the truth. I was ashamed.' His daughter wanted to take him back with her, but he refused to leave. We have had several similar cases . . ."

In Australia

Mother Teresa's helping hand reached out to the poor and was extending to all parts of the world. One day in 1969 there arrived from Australia a certain Mr. John McGee, who had lots of money to give to the poor. On this occasion there was a discussion on the possibility of opening a house of the Missionaries of Charity in Australia, a house for the aborigines who still live in a state bordering on pure nature, and are rejected by society.

The bishop of Broken Hill, Msgr. Warren, officially invited Mother Teresa and her Sisters to establish themselves in his diocese. She went to visit the place alone, in April 1969, then returned with some Sisters in September. The first house for the natives was opened in a place called Bourke.

Mother Teresa was later called on by the archbishop of Melbourne, Cardinal Knox, who had known her well in Calcutta.

The Sisters began by looking for the poor in the streets, as they did in India, but they found none. Then they began visiting the families, asking if there were any poor or elderly people in need of help, but found none. The people were leery at first, because they were not familiar with this type of Sisters. They almost looked down on them. However, the Sisters did not give up. Day after day they meditated, consulted, prayed, and sought in every way to break down the wall of diffidence.

In Australia the problems were not the same as in India. The biggest job was with the drug users, the alcoholics, people alone in the world, and the aged.

The first initiative was to open a house for the rehabilitation of drug addicts and alcoholics, for small children, for juvenile criminals, for released convicts, and so on. The house was blessed by Cardinal Knox in 1973, in the presence of many friends and benefactors.

Mother Teresa had given the first Sisters the following recommendations.

"I do not want you to make miracles in unsettling ways. I prefer that you make mistakes, but do it gracefully. If you do not seek to bring Christ to these people you will be wasting your time."

In Bangladesh (until 1972 known as East Pakistan)

East Pakistan, today Bangladesh, is a country of poor people struggling with enormous economic and social problems.

Between 1970 and 1971 times were difficult in Bangladesh, when two men struggled to win power. The ones who suffered the most were the women and girls, victims of the constant violence. Orphans and the aged also had a lot to endure. The harsh conditions that obtained during the war and afterwards, the various epidemics, including leprosy, made life, already wretched enough, totally insupportable. Several million persons left East Pakistan and took refuge in neighboring countries, India especially, where they hoped to be able to live. This made things even more difficult for India, which already had enough problems of her own to face. So refugee camps were set up.

Mother Teresa did not remain indifferent to this new situation. She went with some Sisters to see what she could do in these refugee camps. At this time there came to Calcutta the American Senator, Edward Kennedy. The Indian government had prepared a program for his visit; instead, he wished to examine the situation in person, and asked if he could visit a refugee camp. The people in charge of the camp, and the refugees themselves, swarmed around him wherever he went, so that he really could not see much of anything. At one place he noticed a Sister who was washing the laundry from the cholera-infested zone. This was Sister Agnes, Mother Teresa's first recruit. The Senator wanted to shake hands with her, but "My hands are not clean" she exclaimed. But he insisted, "As far as I am concerned, the dirtier they are the more honor they deserve. What you are doing here is nothing short of marvelous." The journalist Desmond Doig, from the newspaper *Statesman* who was present at the scene, declared that he would never forget it.

When early in December 1971 India declared war on Pakistan, and backed independence for East Pakistan, from eight to ten million people, refugees in India, left and went back to their homeland, the newly established country of Bangladesh.

The new president, Rahman, personally asked Mother

91

Teresa to open some houses especially for girls who had been raped, and for their children. Thus, as early as the beginning of 1972 the Sisters had opened various houses in Bangladesh, at Khulna and Dacca. Many women, after being raped, had committed suicide out of shame; others had killed their own children soon after giving birth, or had procured abortions. Others too, following the Hindu custom, had been driven from their families. Mother Teresa rose up in their defense, championing life. "For the birth of every child is a sign that God has not grown tired" (Rabindranath Tagore).

Once again, the Sisters of Mother Teresa had passed the test of goodness and love amid inhuman conditions, in those camps where death, misery and hunger reigned supreme. The helpless, like all the others, could bear eyewitness to an infinite love, a love that knows no distinctions.

In Jordan

In June, 1970, the Sisters had begun work in the capital of Jordan, Amman, and in 1973 at Gaza in Israel. In both places they sought to succor the Palestinians who lived surrounded by the fires of hatred and war, which were gradually destroying them. The Sisters declared: "The Muslims were truly very cordial towards us. They called us *hadji* because we wore white robes, like the pilgrims going to Mecca. They do not, of course, understand what Sisters are, but they respect us. Little by little, we learned their language."

In Yemen

Not long afterwards the Sisters were invited to open a house in Yemen. The invitation came from the head of the government, who had heard of Mother Teresa and of her work.

Yemen is a Muslim country, where no Catholics are to be found, nor priests, nor religious. No Christian symbol is permitted. Six centuries ago the last Christian emblems were done away with.

Mother Teresa accepted the invitation on condition that a Catholic priest also be allowed to come.

"The head of the government promised me to do all he could for the Sisters. The government will help us and back us up in everything. As a sign of his good will he presented me with the 'golden sword.' After six centuries, Christ has come back to these people. The population has accepted us readily, and we have already begun fruitful activity among them."

Along with the other pioneer Sisters there arrived also Sister Gertrude from Bangladesh, another of Mother Teresa's earliest recruits, a very capable person, full of life, and a great worker. She had completed her medical studies. The government welcomed the Sisters most cordially; it built a house for them, and sent them a pair of goats every week, to feed the poor. There had even been talk of building a Catholic church, and the Sisters were asked how it should be constructed, since nobody had any idea of how to do so. But the Sisters declined the offer. All they needed was a simple room, properly arranged to serve as a chapel. A large church might have been considered a provocation; many people still harbored anti-Christian prejudices.

The Sisters' work was mainly in caring for the lepers, who were dispersed in various abandoned villages.

One Sister relates:

"Now things are going very well. At first we were afraid to enter the villages of the lepers; it was like in the film 'Ben Hur.' It was not easy to penetrate there. We made our way through knee high piles of manure. There weren't any houses, just caves hollowed out from the mountain side. When they saw us coming they took refuge inside. The babies were frightened to death. Everyone was full of mud. We made them signs with our hands, but they would not draw near us. Finally, Sister Gertrude managed to make contact with them. Personally, I found it repugnant to have to pass through all those heaps of garbage. We needed to make major changes in the way these people lived. With the help of the government we first of all opened a road, so that the garbage could be removed. Next, houses were built, surrounded by nice gardens and flower beds. We taught the children some hygiene. At the beginning, just about everybody was sick. Today, the village has changed its aspect completely. Out of nothing a garden has arisen. The children are happy; it is a pleasure to go among them. And they love us.

"Some of the girls wanted to join us, but it is not a simple matter. Their parents marry them off to boys whom they do not even know. For many, this is something intolerable. They would like to live like us, for God and for their neighbor. They even told their parents this, but it is not an easy matter to convince them. We have to be very prudent because the families, by their hostile attitude, might cause the ruin of all our work. We allow these girls to work with us during the day, then in the evening we send them home. They really help us a great deal. We are only five, and there is so much to be done.

In England

Every house of the Missionaries of Charity has its own story. Here are a few words about the one in London. Mother Teresa herself tells us about it:

"We were looking for a house in London to open the first novitiate in Europe. It was rather difficult. After many fruitless endeavors, we found out that a certain lady was disposed to sell a building which seemed appropriate for us. The price was 6,500 pounds, and had to be paid in cash. The Sisters began going about visiting persons, families and sick people, speaking of our life and activity. We were even invited to address the public over the radio. At once, donations began coming in from all sides. One evening we began counting it all up, and to our great surprise we found that we had exactly 6,500 pounds. Next morning we went to pay for the house. Divine providence is with us always.

"This happened on December 8, 1970, feast of the Immaculate Conception. Around this house live many immigrants from India. This was our first novitiate in Europe, for vocations from Europe and America; the second novitiate, after the one in Calcutta. Today it is in Rome, the center of the Catholic Church."

In time, a second house was opened in London. The Sisters' main occupation is to care for the sick and the aged, and especially the drug addicts and the alcoholics.

"One evening in London," Mother Teresa told us, "the phone rang. It was the police. 'Mother Teresa,' they said, 'we have here a woman who is drunk, and wants to see you. She won't move until you come.' So, I left immediately with another Sister to go and get her. When she saw me from a distance she opened her arms, and happy as a lark asked me: 'Mother Teresa, isn't it true that God is really good? He changed water into wine so that we might have something to drink!' "

Such incidents tell us about the specific problems of our modern world.

In Ireland

In recent years Ireland has seen much bloodshed, especially in northern Ireland, or Ulster. While Mother Teresa was in London she heard of the civil war and of the consequent sufferings endured by people. She called together in Dublin some four hundred of her collaborators and told them of her intention to open a house in Belfast. This soon took place. There was stark poverty to contend with. Without wasting any time the Sisters got to work with the aged and with the many widows: mothers who in the war had lost their husbands and often enough their sons as well. Little children, orphans, and many others found in Mother Teresa and her Sisters new mothers, and the moral support they needed.

In Africa

The first house was opened at Tabora in Tanzania, on September 8, 1968, the feast of Our Lady's nativity. Someone remarked: "How beautiful it is! They came from India to Africa, not to take, but to give."

The first contingent was composed of five Indian Sisters. Their house was unimposing to look at, with a straw roof, just like all the others. People called them "our" Sisters.

Soon there were seven Sisters, one of whom was a medical doctor, something very important in a region where many dangerous diseases were endemic.

Later, in 1972, a house was opened in Mauritius, an island over one thousand miles from Madagascar. Then another one in Addis Ababa, in Ethiopia. Here is how this last house was founded.

Ethiopia had been stricken by a terrible drought which brought with it enormous damage and many deaths. At that moment Mother Teresa was busy organizing a leprosarium in Yemen. She took with her Sister Frederica, who relates that they stopped for three days in Addis Ababa. The local bishop helped them to realize the possibilities for living and working in the city itself. The government too was agreeable. So, on November 23, 1973, the house in the capital was opened.

On the subject of Africa Mother Teresa remarked:

"Africa is a continent materially poor, but spiritually rich. Poor, but offering great opportunities for the apostolate. This inspires great hopes. The outlook for the Church is excellent. And we too can see great changes for development."

In North America

Today the Missionaries of Charity are to be found even in North America. This may appear strange, since they work only with the poor. But the Sisters, as they had in the so-called prosperous countries of Europe, found much to do, even in New York.

"Poverty is everywhere; here it is perhaps worse because there are people who are neither accepted nor loved," says Mother Teresa. Here too the Sisters do what they do everywhere else: they visit the poor, care for the sick, educate the children of the poor, and contend with discrimination.

So far we have outlined the initial expansion of the Sisters in the five continents, but there are many other regions where they work and are expanding, with their houses and institutions.

"I know all my Sisters," says Mother Teresa, and that is how she operates. "I am in touch with all of them. I try to go and visit them as often as I can, even though my visits are spaced out more and more because of the ever increasing number of houses. I often write to them, and they answer me. Although scattered, we remain a family."

Now let us relate how the Missionaries of Charity opened houses at Zagreb and at Skopje, Mother Teresa's home town.

The Sisters in Zagreb

On June 8, 1978, I walked into the cathedral of Zagreb. A group of faithful were saying the rosary. I joined them, and noted several Sisters dressed in Indian *saris.* They were Mother Teresa's Sisters, and she herself was with them. I had heard that on this day they were to open their first house in Yugoslavia, at Zagreb. That was why I had gone there. Mother Teresa led the prayers. After this I approached her, and she recognized me. "What are you doing here?" she inquired. I told her that I had come for the inauguration of her new house, and to celebrate Mass for all the Albanian Catholics in Zagreb and its environs. I invited her to join us if she could. "Very willingly; but first we have to make arrangements with the people who organized this, and with Archbishop Kuharic." She asked for information about the archbishop's residence, about the priests and the people.

"Don't think that I have forgotten my own people. I hope that soon, maybe next year, I can open another house in Yugoslavia, and it will be in our Skopje. I thank you for the newspaper *Drita* which I receive regularly. I am very happy that it is still being published; in this way I still have some connection with the Archdiocese. Keep on sending it to me. May the Lord repay you and bless you. Continue the work, I urge you." At the end she told me:

"We will see each other again tomorrow, or Sunday at the Mass for the Albanians. But I can't speak the language any more. I haven't practiced it for fifty years!" I told her, "Mother, you speak the language of the soul, which all men everywhere understand." She looked at me gently and said: "You are right; that language alone can bring us all together."

Next day in the cathedral a solemn Mass was celebrated. The archbishop of Zagreb spoke in his homily of the importance of vocations in our day; at the end he addressed Mother Teresa and invited her to speak to all the people.

She spoke as she always does, with joy and love, stressing the fact that her own mother had opposed her entry into the convent to the very end. "When she finally consented, she told me: 'All right, my child, go; but always remain God's servant and Christ's.' If I am not faithful to my vocation I shall be judged by my mother, not by God. Some day she is going to ask me, 'My daughter, have you lived for God alone?' "

On Sunday, June 10, 1978, there was a solemn Mass celebrated by Msgr. Michael Cecchini, the Apostolic Nuncio in Belgrade, together with Archbishop Kuharic, his vicar, Bishop Skvore, and a large number of other priests and religious. This was a thanksgiving Mass for the fidelity shown by the Croatian people to the Catholic Church and the Holy See, over a period of thirteen centuries. It was also celebrated in honor of the arrival of the Missionaries of Charity in Zagreb. On this occasion the archbishop presented Mother Teresa, an Albanian, to the people, and with her four of her Sisters who had opened a house in Zagreb. Another of them was also an Albanian, Sister Martha Kerhanaj, from Zjum, the first Albanian who had joined Mother Teresa in her Company.

That afternoon there was the official blessing of the house: a modest little house, the kind Mother Teresa usually wants, situated behind the cathedral.

That day Mother Teresa declared: "My Sisters will remain here to work for the poor who have nothing and nobody. They are the people who are especially ours, since Jesus said: 'I was hungry, and thirsty, I had no home, and you gave me all of that.' We have not come here as social workers; we shall work here, as we do all over the world, for the love of Christ and his mercy."

A conversation with Mother Teresa's Sisters at Zagreb

The Saturday before Mission Sunday in 1979, at Zagreb, not far from the cathedral, I went to greet the Sisters and to congratulate them on the great honor that had come to them: Mother Teresa's being awarded the Nobel Peace Prize.

There were at this time four Sisters in Zagreb: the superioress, Sister Silvia, an Indian; Sister Joselette, also an Indian; Sister Frances, a Belgian; and the helper Sister Kerhanaj, an Albanian from Zjum in the Province of Kosova. I put some questions to them:

You have been in Zagreb for a while; what do you do?

Sister Silvia: I have been here since June 10; that makes four months. We do the same things here as everywhere else: we take care of the aged, the poor, the sick. We have been joyfully surprised by the warm welcome, the faith, the patience, the spirit of sacrifice we have found here. Our patients never complain; on the contrary they show concern for each other. They also assist us to find others who need our help, and things of that sort. They welcome us, and treat us as though they were our parents; they warn us to pay attention to dangers, tell us not to work too hard, and to take care of ourselves.

Have you come across any difficulties up to now?

Sister Silvia: I can say that there are difficulties everywhere. In particular, I can say this: here we go out to find the sick and the abandoned only when others tell us of their needs. Then we go out seeking for them. In other places we would go looking from house to house. Hence, this is for us a new mode of operating. We have to locate the needy first, and then help them.

What were you expecting when you arrived at Zagreb, a better or a worse situation?

Sister Silvia: I did not even suspect that there are so many good Christians here. Nor had I expected this kind of work. I was pleasantly surprised.

The work done by Mother Teresa and her Company has been recognized by the awarding of the Nobel Peace Prize. What were your reactions when you heard about this?

Sister Silvia: Nothing in particular. If this is God's will, so much the better. Most especially, we are glad because this recognition shows that humanity appreciates Mother Teresa's work. In a word, even today people are sensitive to poverty, to goodness, to the poor, and to love. We are grateful to the poor who make it possible for us to do this work. Our task is a lot easier than what they have to bear.

Sister Silvia, allow me a personal question. Why did you choose the Order of the Missionaries of Charity, and when did you join?

Sister Silvia: I entered in 1964, wanting to be a poor missionary. Two of my aunts were members of the Order, and through them I came to know Mother Teresa. I was fortunate enough to entertain her in my house, and this was another element in my vocation.

Sister Ancilla: I entered in 1976. I always wanted to serve the poor.

What is Mother Teresa for you?

Sister Silvia: How can I explain it in a few words? For me, she is our mother; that says it all. She is an exemplary Sister, a saint, a truly great woman. When I am with her I feel truly happy. I have no problems; I feel secure and at peace. But I really can't explain it.

Sister Ancilla: I met Mother Teresa for the first time in April, 1977, in Rome, when I was a postulant. On this first occasion she gave me the impression of being a humble Sister. This touched me deeply. So did her love for people, great love for everyone. So did her manner of speaking, her interest in each one of us. She taught me how to live entirely for God and with God, how to unite myself every day more closely to Him and also to Our Lady. Her prayer pleased me immensely, and also her manner of living every day with God.

Do you remember some special encounter, some message of hers?

Sister Ancilla: Yes, there were many such, but I remember some in particular. I remember how she spoke to us of the novitiate, how nothing should separate us from God, neither people, nor big things, nor little things. "If you are thinking of not becoming saints it would be better for you to leave now, in peace, as you came. It is necessary to live in holiness, serenely. Everything you do must be done with love, so that it may be great before God, for he is love."

This Peace Prize is a message for the entire Church; is it one also for the Church in Albania?

Sister Silvia: Every epoch has had its saints, who upheld the Church, like St. Francis and others. Mother Teresa is entirely tranquil, even though she is aware of the general situation of the Church, especially in Albania. She has dedicated herself entirely to God; for her, God is the only true reality. She lives with God, and hence difficulties do not upset her. She just has faith.

Sister Ancilla: At first I did not know much about the situation in Albania, and even now I am not too well informed. I only know that there religion is not free. Our bishop recommended to me to pray for the conversion of Albania. This I do every day. I think that some day the free profession of the faith will come back there too. Up to now we have not had many Albanian saints. From what one can see, Mother Teresa will become our great saint who will help us a great deal. God has chosen her to offer hope to our people, to the Church, and to each one of us. I am happy that among us too there are such holy Sisters. This Prize will afford courage to many, will sustain our faithful people and help them persevere in their faith, so that God may always be with us, and we need not be afraid of anything.

Up to now, how many sick or poor or abandoned people have you met with in Zagreb?

Sister Silvia: A great many; more than a hundred by far. Furthermore, every evening someone comes here for adoration; five or ten people come to pray with us. Many are interested in our manner of living. Fifteen or twenty young people have been attracted, and observe us closely. It would seem that they feel the tug of a vocation.

Chapter 7
The Grain of Mustard Seed Becomes a Tree

The Missionary Brothers of Charity

As we follow in detail the growth of Mother Teresa's work, even without intending to do so, we think of Jesus' parable about the grain of mustard seed: it is the smallest of all seeds, but once it has been planted, it grows and becomes the largest plant in the garden, and eventually turns into a tree which offers its branches to the birds of the air, which come and build their nests in it (Mt 13:31-32).

Where did her work begin? When and where did the seed first fall onto the good soil?

Questioned by some journalists, Teresa once answered thus:

"It started many years ago, when I was still at Skopje in Yugoslavia. I was barely twelve years old. . . . We children went to a non-Catholic school, but we had some very fine priests who helped young people to follow their vocations as indicated by God. It was then that I realized for the first time that my vocation was to serve the poor. This was in 1922."

We have rapidly sketched the dynamic development of the Sisters' community. We shall now dwell briefly on another, parallel branch of the company; then on the external collaborators, and finally on the ascetical communities.

In Mother Teresa's history we find that the archbishop of Calcutta, on March 25, 1963, feast of the Annunciation, gave her permission to start the male counterpart of her Company, the Missionary Brothers of Charity; and that in less than two years this had become a moral entity of papal right (1965).

This community did not spring out of nothing, nor did it easily reach the stage of standing on its own two feet. We have seen how many girls were attracted in an irresistible manner to Mother Teresa. The same thing happened for a number of

102

boys and young men. When they joined her she had work for them to do. She thus recalls the start of this undertaking.

"At Calcutta, in a certain area of the city where our Sisters worked, they had discovered, in a Catholic parish, a group of people who, to all appearances, had no connection with the Church. None of them attended any religious ceremonies; the children had not made their first communion; many adults lived together without having been married. The Sisters wanted to remedy this situation. Similar cases were to be found in other poor quarters too. We came upon many couples living together without having been married regularly in church. The Sisters began gathering the papers needed to regularize these marriages. Unfortunately, the priests did not always cooperate with us too well. We keenly felt the need for a priest who understood what we were trying to do, who wanted to second the Sisters' efforts, and might himself take a hand in solving these problems. Then it might be possible for us to do something more.

"I realized that the situation was complicated. We had to follow the rules of Church law, but certain of these unions were permanent. In Calcutta, as in other large cities, people came in from the country looking for work. They left wife (or husband) and children at home. With time, in the new surroundings, they formed relationships with other persons who came to the house, or cooked, or did other things of the kind. From these unions there were born children, innocent although they were illegitimate; and we had to help them. I needed some helpers among the priests."

Faced with these problems, Mother Teresa turned to Fr. Edward Le Joly, but he was already too busy with other activities, and, as he said, he was not really prepared to handle such delicate cases. Teresa foresaw that in the future things could get even more complicated, if some young man were brought into the house while the "husband" was at work. This could give rise to doubts, suspicions, and jealousy, with consequences that no one could foresee.

This is how she began. A few priests were the first to take interest in the matter, and then she got other helpers who were lay people. But these never did achieve the success obtained by the Missionary Sisters of Charity. Moreover, at the beginning, and for nearly three years, Mother Teresa personally directed this group of people, a situation which ran into considerable difficulties. Catholic tradition did not accept the idea that a woman could be the superior of a male community. But when a young Australian missionary came along, the Jesuit Ian Travers-Ball, today known as Brother Andrew, things began to look up.

"I was getting ready to make my final vows," he told me, "and was stationed at Sitagarh. I was obsessed by the problem of the poor. I asked myself what I could do for them. My superiors then sent me along with other Brothers, to help out in the *Shish Bhavan*—the Boys' Village. When I came back to Sitagarh I sought advice from Fr. Schillebeeckx, our master. He right away approved my plan to join the Brothers who were helping the Sisters. The Jesuit provincial of Calcutta likewise gave his consent. We contacted the superior general in Rome, for his approval, and for permission to live outside of the community (exclaustration). In a few weeks the question was resolved. All the Jesuits were very understanding and gave me a lot of help."

When he joined the new community, Ian changed his name to Andrew.

Once, when I asked him why he had decided to change the direction of his vocation he replied: "The needs were so obvious."

His former fellow-religious in Australia think that they lost one of the best members of the community; but he never had any doubts about the matter.

At first the modest group of Brothers was not recognized as a religious community, even though they lived a life much like that of the Sisters: taking the same vows, and dedicating their lives to relieving the sufferings of the poorest among the poor in a spirit of joyful and serene activity.

Brother Andrew tells us more:

"So long as there were only a few aspirants, Rome did not want to grant permission for the new institute, even though the archbishop of Calcutta himself recommended it. The reply was that first of all more candidates had to be found, then permission would be granted. It was a vicious circle. If we operated without permission, we would not have any candidates, since the priests would not send us any until we got official approval from Rome; at the same time, before giving us canonical approval Rome wanted to see a larger number of members. But we were insistent, and kept showing the situation in its real colors; and in the end we won out."

At the start there were nine of them.

But not all the problems were resolved as yet. Another was to determine who would be the superior. At the beginning, the superior was Mother Teresa herself, with the help of Fr. Henry, who lent her a hand in difficult times.

However, Brother Andrew also felt a "vocation within a vocation" and followed it courageously. His story was like that of Mother Teresa herself. She describes it briefly as follows:

"I think that he reflected a long time over the idea of dedicating himself completely to the poor. He is a saint, a truly holy man. He is a virtuous Jesuit in every way—physical, spiritual and intellectual. The two of us had the same inspiration. It is strange. We are different. Obviously, he is far better than I; he is truly holy. He was not our first Brother. The Brothers started in March 1963, whereas Brother Andrew joined in 1965. It is a remarkable coincidence that the Brothers began their activity at Calcutta the very day on which he was ordained at Hazaribagh, the Australian missionary center, March 25, 1963. In 1964 he came to visit us, to see what we were doing. After that, he had no further doubts about what he should do. He followed his vocation."

Meanwhile other vocations for the Brothers began coming in from all parts of India, mainly from Chota Nagpur and Kerala, a few from Bengal, from Bombay, and even from the West, especially from the United States. Later on, they went to work in Vietnam and in Hong Kong, in Formosa, in Japan, in South Korea, and Macao.

Their life was not an easy one, for it demanded much renunciation and a great spirit of prayer. Not all could measure up. The number of those who quit was greater than among the Sisters. One Brother declared:

"When I entered the novitiate in 1967 there were thirteen

of us; two years later when we made first vows, we were seven; and in 1975 only four made final vows."

The Indian journalist, Doig, thus described the Brothers' vow ceremony.

"I witnessed a liturgy impressive in its simplicity. No flowers, no banners, no varicolored bunting. There was not even any electric light, and the inside of the church was in shadow, even though outside the summer sun shone brightly. Some of the Brothers, including two foreigners, were making their solemn vows. Parents and friends were present, and from the niches in the walls the solemn statues of the saints looked down. I was sitting next to a group of Brothers who did not yet have any vows, and who formed the choir. The chants were accompanied on the harmonium and Indian drums. They were joyful and pleasing to the ear.

"After Mass, in the midst of the joyful confusion of greetings and good wishes, Mother Teresa introduced me to Brother Aloysius, a lad with a charming smile, from South India. He was with his family which had come to Calcutta for the occasion. The women wore the *sari* of the south, brilliantly dyed, and held bouquets of flowers in their hands. They all wore flowers in their hair except two, who wore the *sari* of the Missionaries of Charity. The mother told me, with pride and joy, that both of these nuns were Aloysius' own sisters. They had had another sister but she was dead; and it was for this that her brother, at the time a student in northern India, had decided to join the Missionary Brothers of Charity and had taken her name. That morning, under the Indian sun, there was no happier family anywhere. Mother Teresa observed them with love and pride, which, on such an occasion, nobody could blame her for. 'Isn't it marvelous?' she inquired."

The task of the Missionary Brothers is to work where the Sisters cannot go, or where it would be extremely difficult for them to do so. In the houses for the dying at Calcutta they take care of the men, while the Sisters for the most part deal with the women. The Brothers also look after the orphans, the crippled, the abandoned children, and the severely handicapped. Many work among the lepers. In the western world they care for alcoholics, drug addicts and abandoned old people. One of the Brothers in California thus described their activity:

"At Los Angeles we have four communities, with over twenty Brothers. We work among the poor Hispanic families. We visit the needy, we run a center where the women can come to sew and thus make clothes for their families; they also get vegetables, bread and other foodstuffs donated by various stores in the city. When we can, we take care of a small group of abandoned children, or youngsters who have run away from home, until they are able to get along on their own. In addition, we provide for twenty or so older citizens without homes. They can come to us for a place to sleep, for clothes and other necessities. But the truly important thing is that with us they can find a place where they are accepted, wanted, and loved. Even though it is a rather unusual one, this for them *is a home*. Besides this, over fifty people come here daily to eat their main meal. We also have a novitiate in the city. Our candidates come from five states. Half the day they work with the other Brothers among the needy; they visit the aged and the sick, the alcoholics, the old couples who live in hospices. In short, they spend their time where violence and alienation are everyday occurrences.

"Our work is too modest compared with the overwhelming misery around us. Our work is much like what we do in Calcutta. In both cities many people die neglected and abandoned: in Calcutta, on the streets; in Los Angeles, in the slums. They are all either lepers who really have that disease, or who just suffer from social leprosy: the alcoholics, the delinquents, the abandoned children. Sometimes we are overwhelmed, realizing how feeble our efforts are compared with the immense needs. For us, it is a blessing to see an apparently incurable person recover his health; a poor fellow unexpectedly become rich in a most unimaginable manner. We are grateful because here we give food to Jesus who is hungry and thirsty; we clothe him and protect him when he is freezing and homeless, we embrace him and love him when he is alone and discouraged."

Over the years the Brothers have gathered an enormous amount of experience, rich with touching encounters. Here is one, as the superior general, Brother Andrew, relates it:

"Some years ago a man died in Calcutta, one of the most successful men I have ever known. I mentioned him in my letters. When he was five years old he used to play around my table where I was trying to write. He had a stiff leg, and sometimes suffered spells of insanity. The Sisters had found him in the street. 'My name is Johnny Walker,' he said, and so that was what we called him. He had been abandoned when very small, and had remained a cripple with limited intelligence. Still, he was happy and content, always ready to sing and dance and amuse everyone else. He never got angry. I spoke of him in Malcolm Muggeridge's book, *Something Beautiful for God.* I related how with his sad stories he amused the little ones so that they might forget their own misfortunes. Thousands of people have heard about him. Every day he prayed with the other children, and on Sundays he also went to Mass, joining his hands and bowing his head. He knew that God was there; he knew that love, joy and smiles are in God. Johnny died at the age of eighteen; he had a sudden attack and drowned in shallow water. After a happy and successful life he now is a saint, if anyone ever deserved that name. Just thinking of Johnny's life and death strengthens me and gives joy to me and to all those to whom I relate his story."

Brother Andrew thus explains the guiding thought behind his work:

"I believe in the God of history because nothing else in the world is as solid and stable. Everything can fall apart, and you can find yourself trapped in the debris of a ruined life, in a situation from which there is no escape. Then all of us will finally be poor and free. The love of God and his mercy remain forever; in this contrasting reality one is conscious of this; conscious that there is nothing but this. . . ."

To someone who was starting to write about the Brothers, Brother Andrew gave this advice: "You need to debunk everything that they have written about us and our work. What is written certainly influences the readers positively, but sometimes we have to spend six months trying to correct the distorted views that our aspirants have acquired by reading various publications about us.

"Say that we are ordinary people, all of us; that we have our defects, limits and weaknesses, like the Sisters, Mother Teresa included. We two do not always see eye to eye; sometimes we argue. We are just means, not really fit for the job we have to do; but the miracle is that God took us, just as we are, for his work, and that through us he does so much good."

To be on the lips of everyone is sometimes a catastrophe. It is certainly dangerous. Humility and the conviction of one's evangelical nothingness are the basis of the work of the Missionary Brothers of Charity.

Mother Teresa's co-workers

As the work grew, various collaborators gathered around Mother Teresa. We have already spoken of the Missionary Brothers and Sisters. Now we must say something about those whom she herself called her "second self." She divides them into three groups: the simple co-workers, the sick or suffering co-workers, and the contemplatives.

The first group can be found all over the world. They are directed by Ms. Ann Blaikie of Great Britain (Southhall, Middlesex). Elsewhere, as in France, they are called "The Friends of Mother Teresa."

"It all started during a difficult pregnancy," relates Ann Blaikie, "when I was working with other people in a store called 'The Helpful Union' in Calcutta. We sold women's handiwork to help the missions. I was pregnant, but I still had to carry on with the business. One afternoon, I was sitting on the balcony; it was hot, and I was asking myself how I could still make myself useful in this world. All of a sudden an idea struck me . . . go and talk with Mother Teresa. I had never met her, but I had accidentally read in the newspaper some information about her; and besides I remembered that one of my friends was in contact with her."

It was during the summer of 1954, and the day of her patron saint's feast, July 26. Ann and her friend went to the first hospital opened by Mother Teresa. The latter received them cordially and brought them to the hospital for the dying at Kalighat. While on the way, they agreed to collect toys for the annual Christmas festival which was being promoted in the press at Calcutta. Delighted with this, Ann asked whether it might be possible to collect a little money too, to buy for the Christian children at Christmas some clothes, shirts and shoes. A dozen European ladies went to work enthusiastically; they made playthings and little angels out of tissue paper, which they then sold in order to raise the money needed. In fact, at Christmastime the children received the clothing they needed and the second hand toys which had been repainted. After Christmas, the ladies met Mother Teresa again to discuss what they had done. They had congratulated themselves over it, and wanted to hear her opinion.

"When she arrived," relates one of the ladies, "she thanked us, and immediately added that now we needed to think of clothes and toys for another feast, the one for the Muslim children. Then, after that, there would come the feast of the Hindu children." The women were impressed by Mother Teresa's appeal that they should do something more than just an occasional gesture of generosity. The plight of so many of the youngsters was extremely serious; they were struck by what could be called her "ecumenical sense" in solving practical problems. It was not enough for them to help their own poor children; they should think of all of them without any distinction.

For the Catholics that was the Marian Year, recalling the centenary of the proclamation of the dogma of the Immaculate Conception of Mary (1854-1954), and because of this the group of benefactresses began calling themselves the Marian Society. At first, they did not limit themselves to helping Mother Teresa only, but worked to support the missions in general. Gradually they made their way into the circles of Indian and Anglo Indian society, Catholic and non-Catholic, and their activity extended more and more. When Mother Teresa began working with the lepers, these ladies helped her by procuring and collecting bandages and medicines, and by taking care of the packaging and forwarding of these materials.

As for the new developments in the enterprise, Ms. Blaikie writes:

"In 1960 some of us returned to England. God arranged it

that we happened to live fairly close to each other, perhaps within a radius of twenty-five or thirty miles. I had not been home a month when Mr. John Southworth, at the time the director of the Society for helping the lepers, got me involved again. He had sent some money to Mother Teresa, and she had answered, telling him to get in touch with me, since I could give him useful advice. Six months later she came to London in person, and made an appeal on TV for the lepers. From this modest beginning there sprang the union of her co-workers in the United Kingdom. John Southworth became its president, I its vice president, and other old Indian hands members of its board of directors.

"The work of the group consists in prayer, and in explaining to the other members how they can help. They can prepare bandages, gather used clothes to send to India, or sell them and send the money thus brought in. In all cases we made it a point to stress that the important thing was how much love they put into this task, and not the amount of money collected. Four or five years later, when Mother Teresa returned to England and could see for herself the misery existing here, she asked the collaborators to help the poor in their own neighborhoods. It was thus that the society spread throughout the country. Today the collaborators work in hospitals, care for the mentally retarded, visit the aged, and so on.

"Besides this we have improved our life of prayer. In many cities and countries the collaborators organize prayer groups. Ours in this area meets in the home of one of our members who suffers from arthritis and cannot move; she spends her life in a wheelchair, with a husband who is an epileptic. We gather there every month. They are the contact between us and those who help the sick and suffering.

"All over England days of recollection (sometimes several days) take place, especially on weekends. The whole enterprise is strongly ecumenical in character, because the collaborators belong to various denominations and religions.

"Besides the three vows of religion the Missionaries take a fourth vow, to serve Christ gratuitously and wholeheartedly under the appearance of the most wretched and most miserable. We collaborators apply this vow during our life.

Mother Teresa bases the life of her collaborators on prayer. Our prayer amounts to the same as that of her Missionaries. Also, when we meet, we always start the prayer by two or three minutes of recollection. She also wants us to gather once a month for an hour's prayer. From these encounters the collaborators return to their everyday work, showing their love for their families, their neighborhood, the people in their area, the entire nation, and the whole world."

In the 1950s in the United States the National Council of Catholic Women began seconding the work of Mother Teresa by an annual contribution to the fund "Madonna Plan," under the patronage of the Catholic Relief Services, which is the American Catholic organization for help to the Church overseas. Since this group regularly informs public opinion about the destination of the contributions received, the work of Mother Teresa became ever better known. The CRS and the National Council of Catholic Women were connected through the work of Ms. Eileen Egan, in charge of the relief going to India, and an old friend of Mother Teresa's.

Towards the end of the 1950s and all during the 60s more and more was written in the newspapers about Mother Teresa. She had become a person of worldwide fame. This was a major reason why in 1969 the International Association of Co-Workers of Mother Teresa was founded and aggregated to the Missionaries of Charity, and its rule approved by Pope Paul VI.

The sick and suffering collaborators

Those of whom we have been speaking did not belong to the first group of her collaborators. These were found among the weakest, right at the start of the Company.

In 1948, Mother Teresa was at Patna, preparing herself for her new vocation. There, in the same hospital she met a young Belgian girl, Jacqueline de Decker. The latter at first wanted to join Mother Teresa in her new undertaking, but she got seriously ill, and after two years in India, had to go back home.

"Since I was seventeen I longed to dedicate myself to God through serving the poor in India," she declared. "There were eight of us who shared this same ideal. Then the war separated us. A Jesuit asked me to accept a position as a doctor at Madras in India. The day I left, December 31, 1946, he died suddenly; but the bishop of Madras convinced me to learn the language and the customs of the Hindus. So for a while I worked in the convalescent wards and taught the other nurses. I even helped to organize Gandhi's villages."

Jacqueline de Decker got a doctorate in sociology from the Catholic University of Louvain. At the same time she also obtained a diploma in nursing and in first aid. During the war she had helped the British army, in the bombarded cities, most of which had been abandoned by other doctors. Even today the people in Antwerp remember how young Jacqueline went about among the wounded, the afflicted, those needing help. Even though she had been trained in such a school, she admits that faced with the misery she found in India she felt surprised and ill prepared. The horrendous poverty surrounding her all but destroyed her.

"They advised me to get in touch with Mother Teresa, but she was in Patna for a three-month course in first aid. That is where I met her. She was in the chapel, all wrapped up in prayer. We spoke for a moment, and found that we both had the same ideal. We worked together in the hospitals of Patna and of Mokameh, then, at the end of November, Mother Teresa returned to Calcutta. In my address book you can still see 'Mother Teresa, 14 Creek Lane, Calcutta.' All her letters came to me from there."

Medical advice obtained in Belgium showed that her health was uncertain; various spots in her spinal column risked bringing on paralysis. And these forced her to undergo operations. She submitted to a first operation, then to several others. She always hoped to be able to return to India, but this hope vanished like snow in the sun. At first she thought that it was God's will for her to dedicate herself to the poor people in India, but she came to realize that such was not the case. She fell into deep depression, convinced that she had failed, and that she was abandoned by God in whom she had placed all her trust ever since her early years. From this great trial, however, she learned one thing: every experience, no matter how negative, can always teach us something good and spiritually constructive. Her faith returned, and she realized that God had not abandoned her, but had given her a different task: joyfully to dedicate her own life, sufferings and trials, to the work of Mother Teresa and of the girls who, like her, desired to become the first missionaries of Christ. In 1952 she received a letter from Mother Teresa:

"You were hoping to become a Missionary. Why do you not bind yourself spiritually to our community, if you love it so much? While we are working in the poor quarters you can share in our merits, in our work and prayer, by your sufferings and your prayer. True, the work here is immense, and I need ever so many pairs of hands, but we also need souls like yours who pray and suffer for the work. Your body will be in Belgium, but your spirit will be in India, where souls are reaching out to God but cannot draw near to him unless someone pays their debts."

So, in her own country, Jacqueline de Decker decided to pay her share of the "debt." Phrases in Teresa's letter, such as, "I need so many people, sick and suffering, who are willing to join the Company as my spiritual children," touched Jacqueline in the depths of her heart, and thus together they founded the "Union for sick and suffering co-workers."

When the first ten novices were about to take vows in 1958, Mother Teresa, through Jacqueline de Decker, expressed the desire that each one should forge a spiritual bond with some sick or suffering person. While she was convalescing after one of the thirty operations she had to undergo, Jacqueline began looking among the patients for those who were willing to accept Mother Teresa's offer: to keep up a spiritual contact with one of the Sisters, to pray for her, and for the other Sisters, to write once or twice a year, and especially to offer with all their hearts the secret of their sufferings, donating it with faith and love for the success of the work going on in that strange, distant land. What was the true meaning of this connection?

Let us answer, in the words of Mother Teresa:

"The purpose of our Company is to satisfy the thirst for love that Jesus on the cross feels for souls, and this we do by laboring for the salvation and the holiness of the needy who live in the slums. It must be a spiritual unity, the spirit of our

Company itself, and this is: to dedicate oneself completely to God in loving faith and perfect joy. Whoever wants to be a Missionary of Charity is welcome, but it is my specific desire that there be joined to you the sick, the paralytics, the lame and those suffering from incurable diseases, because such people will bring many souls into the sight of Jesus."

Those seriously ill, by dedicating themselves and their sufferings to this task, vast and profound as it is, can little by little transform their tragic condition. We read in a letter from one such invalid:

"It is true, I suffer a great deal, but nothing of this treasure is lost. When I cannot go on any more I offer everything, simply, for my little Sister Missionary of Charity. When my back hurts, when it seems to me that my shoulders are welded to my knees, when I experience a painful stiffness at the least movement, which does not allow me to sleep, I begin in thought my trip to India with my little Sister, or to Africa with my young seminarian; then in a Carmel in Madagascar I stop in silence to pay homage to the Lord in the monstrance which I donated. This long trip tires me and helps me fall asleep; I am happy to be able to go to sleep after a night of this kind of missionary activity."

Another invalid, suffering from multiple sclerosis, writes: "Do not the Missionaries do a marvelous work? My pains and sufferings pale into insignificance when I think of what those good Sisters are doing."

Today, throughout the world, there are over two thousand collaborating invalids who have accepted the challenge, and the paradoxical appeal "to love and serve Jesus, not by what they offer, but by what they take." There are many such in England, in Ireland, in western Europe, in Spain, Belgium, France, Luxembourg, Switzerland, Germany, Austria, Italy and Malta, not to mention Denmark and Poland. There are more in India, Japan, the island of Mauritius, South Africa, Canada, the United States, and several countries of South America.

Jacqueline acts as the living link between the International Association of collaborators and sick and suffering members. In spite of her own precarious state of health, which does not even permit her to type, she takes care of a great deal of the correspondence. When Mother Teresa went to Oslo to receive the Nobel Prize, with her was her faithful, constant and unwearingly suffering co-worker, Miss Jacqueline de Decker from Antwerp.

The ascetical communities

The more active work is needed, the more prayer is necessary. This is the principle which governs all Mother Teresa's activity and that of her co-workers; work and prayer are inseparable.This heritage of Christianity is the primitive experience of humanity. The Rule of Saint Benedict in the history of human culture can be summed up in the words: *Ora et labora*. We find the same thought in the ascetical works of St. Basil. Work must be sustained by prayer.

A house of intensive prayer appeared to the eyes of Mother Teresa as a gigantic wellspring of energy, a powerhouse into which those who go about in the world's arena can plug in. The radiation of this energy is intangible, but no less real and powerful for that.

On this basis Mother Teresa founded at New York in 1976 a new branch of her Missionaries of Charity: the Missionary Sisters of the Word. Their special aim is to grasp the word of God through the eucharist and meditation, and then to announce it to his people through their own presence and works of spiritual charity, so that "the word may be made flesh, and dwell among people." This community was founded for those who felt themselves attracted to meditation and prayer, and who also dedicate several hours daily to the practice of the apostolate among the poor.

This is how the superioress in New York describes their life:

"Our convent is in the Bronx. Many people are reluctant to come here, but the Lord chose this place for us. It is the right place indeed, because many poor, desperate people live all around us. We are surrounded by houses that have burned down. But one day a drunk came and asked us for a rosary. Later, he came back, bringing a small bouquet of flowers for the tabernacle. At other times children ring the bell and ask: 'Can we see Jesus?' or 'We want to pray with God.' "

Not long after the founding of these contemplative houses Mother Teresa founded the male ascetical community in Rome. What do they do? They are called the Missionary Brothers of the Word. One of them, a Roman, describes his activity:

"Our average day obviously includes much more than we can write on a sheet of paper. Besides prayer, we spend two or three hours in apostolic activity among the needy, either here at home or outside. We offer comfort, friendship, and prayer together. Following the example of Jesus Christ the Good Shepherd, we go out looking for the lost sheep, bringing them the Good News.

"We seek out the alcoholics and the drug addicts in the streets, or wherever they can be found.

"We look for the sick, abandoned in the hospitals, in homes, or elsewhere.

"We try to find the people living alone, the aged.

"We visit the prisoners even if in the eyes of the world they are criminals. If they are guilty, we try to convince them to ask God for pardon and grace.

"We go to pray with people in the refuges for the abandoned and the homeless, to celebrate the sacrament of reconciliation with them, and every week we have adoration of the Most Blessed Sacrament with them.

"We give courage to the discouraged, we give sight back to the spiritually blind, as we pray with them and for them, accepting them unconditionally as the Father in heaven accepts us, comforting them in their solitude, strengthening them in their difficult trials, and advising them in their moments of doubt.

"In short, we are at the disposal of all those who are in extreme spiritual and material need, when this need is genuine and there is no other place where they can find help."

Two or three hours spent among the needy are the complement and the fruit of profound prayer in which the contemplative Brothers regularly sanctify themselves.

In September 1974, Mother Teresa expressed the desire that every one of her houses should be "spiritually adopted" by one or several ascetical communities of other orders throughout the world. Her intention was that the enclosed orders and monasteries in the Church should sustain, thanks to their own prayers and the retired life they lead, the desire of her Missionaries of Charity to live in the service of the poorest. Thus, thanks to her intervention the French priest and monk, George Gorrée, president of the French co-workers of Mother Teresa and the author of a famous book about her, *Love Knows no Frontiers* (Paris, 1972) took upon himself to work out these connections. In a year he succeeded in finding about 400 monasteries which were glad to accept the task of being spiritual godfathers and godmothers by including in their daily work and prayer the intention of Teresa's missionaries. For the older orders which today suffer from a shortage of vocations, accepting this concrete contact with the youthful and dynamic Company of Teresa, full of candidates both male and female, and without any problems on this score, this was both an incentive and an opportunity to make their own manner of life spring up once more. One of Mother Teresa's collaborators remembers how he was honored in being invited to enter a cloistered convent in order to speak to the Sisters about the work of Mother Teresa. The cordiality shown him on this occasion made an indelible impression on him.

Today, over 450 monasteries in France, Spain, Germany, Belgium, Italy, Luxembourg, England, Canada and the United States have agreed to join in spiritual cooperation with Mother Teresa's work.

One of her missionaries in Calcutta maintains:

"If I can dedicate myself every day to the service of the lepers, it is because somewhere, far away, perhaps in Canada, the contemplative Sisters are praying for me." It seems that modern science confirms the possibility that there can be a real transfer of spiritual energy from being to being.

Mother Teresa also believes that the essence of all the work accomplished up to today from the modest beginnings thirty years ago, is to satisfy the plea of Jesus dying on the cross and saying: "I thirst!" A cross with these words hangs on the wall of the houses and churches of Mother Teresa.

She once explained to her collaborators how she pictures the work to herself:

"We are like the five wounds of Jesus; the right hand are our contemplative Sisters; the left hand, the contemplative Brothers, the right foot, the Missionaries of Charity; the left foot the Missionary Brothers of Charity; his heart, our co-workers. Don't you believe that we can take refuge in his sacred wounds? The contemplatives are his hands because they are joined in prayer; the active Missionaries of Christ are his feet because with them they go everywhere in the world. The collaborators are like his heart because home is the heart of everything, the family, where they truly live. All of us can find comfort in his heart."

From the outset Mother Teresa knew very well that she could do little by herself. Hence she constantly gathered co-workers of both sexes, sympathizers, advisers and benefactors, in addition to those who backed her through their own vocation. "I can do what you cannot; you can do what I cannot; together we can do something beautiful for God." Malcolm Muggeridge used this statement as the title of his book and of the film which, perhaps more than anything else has contributed to the fame of Mother Teresa, and led her to her position in the front ranks of world personalities.

People from all over the world, therefore, seeing that her path led forward, came and followed her. It is worthy of remark that among her first and closest collaborators, the Missionaries of Charity, close to ninety percent were Indians, mostly Catholics. A few years ago, in addition, about eighty Hindu girls who wanted to be accepted into her Company, came to her; they were ready to live a common life, to practice the vows, and to fulfill the other duties of the Sisters even though they did not want to give up being Hindus. Mother Teresa was happy and surprised at their attitude, and would have accepted them willingly, but she did not want to move too quickly. As was her custom, she took advice and referred the matter to Rome, with due explanations. That same year, 1981, she was informed that her request had been accepted. Even non-Christian girls could belong to the Missionaries of Charity on condition that they would accept the Sisters' life-style.

Previously, this was something new, which did not need to

119

be overstressed, but required careful examination, especially as regards the undoubtedly ecumenical tone of this new departure. Perhaps some day deeper studies will show that this all began far earlier, in her childhood at Skopje, where she grew up surrounded by other religious groups. She was born in a country still under Turkish domination, which had been the case in the Balkans since the fourteenth century, and in what is now Yugoslavia, it ceased only on the eve of the First World War (1912). When she was born the supreme chief was the Sultan of Constantinople, Mohammed Reshad V (1909-18). In her native city there were Orthodox Christians, Moslems, Jews, and a Catholic minority which formed a solid spiritual nucleus. When she began work in Calcutta at the age of twenty, the political situation was very different, whereas, from the religious point of view the changes weren't so important. Even there the Catholics were a tiny minority, while the great majority of the people (seventy percent) were Hindus, then Moslems, and then all the Christian religions together. From the day she went out into the streets and began to live her new vocation, even until today, along with her Brothers and Sisters she has always cared for the non-Christians. Their religion did not interest her because in her work she never concerned herself with making conversions or proselytism. She esteemed highly the personal contact, the religious witness given to people and looked upon every human being, needy and suffering, with the eyes of faith in Christ, thirsting for love. Her principal role in her work was to help the Hindus to be good Hindus, and the Moslems to be better Moslems, in their faith in Allah.

Intolerance, like fanaticism is most often an indication of weak faith rather than the opposite. Even certain government officials notoriously hostile to foreign missionaries, to the point of trying to have them expelled from the country, have great respect for Mother Teresa. Although a European by birth in a Balkan country, her fatherland today is India, or rather, the whole world, wherever there are poor people to be helped. She is a real missionary, a prophet of the future, an individual of international distinction.

Chapter 8
Awards and Recognition

From 1962 to 1979

In September 1962, Mother Teresa received from the Indian president the Prize of the Miraculous Lotus. Although this is not the country's highest honor, on this occasion Mother Teresa was for the first time publicly awarded a prize in India. She was also the first person of foreign birth who received this distinction.

In ecclesiastical circles certain doubts were expressed: Archbishop Dyer of Calcutta did not know exactly what to do. Some advised him not to allow Sister Teresa to go and accept the prize because it might make her proud!

Others, who knew her better, assured him categorically: "Your Excellency, do not be concerned. Mother Teresa does not even know what pride is. Tell her that by awarding her this prize the president really wishes to express his gratitude to all the missionaries who serve the poor."

She herself was not sure she should go. "I don't think I shall go to Delhi," she said to the archbishop. He replied: "Mother, you must go."

President Radjendrah Prassad presented her with the award with tears of emotion and gratitude. All those present greeted her with a thunderous round of applause.

Madam Vijayalakshni Pandit, who was present, described the occasion as follows:

"The imposing hall of the Durbar at Rashtrapathi Bhavan fell silent all at once, when a Sister dressed in a *sari* went up to the podium. She took the prize as though it had been a sick child, or a dying person seeking the shelter of her arms. It did not mean anything much different to her. The hall was filled with a strange sensation. All realized that something great, and at the same time something very simple was happening. The head of the government, the late Jawaharlal Nehru, confessed that he could not hide his own deep feelings." Then, the Philippine government on August 31, 1962 awarded the Ramon Magsaysay Prize to Mother Teresa, as "the most meritorious woman in Asia," in recognition of her "cooperation and boundless understanding, as well as for her unceasing work for the poor."

One day Sister Frances, from the city of Agra, phoned Mother Teresa asking for urgent help.

"Mother, I need 50,000 rupees. Over here there is a crying and urgent need to start a house for the children."

Mother Teresa replied: "That is too much, my daughter, I will call you back; for the moment we have nothing. . . ." A short time later the phone rang again. It was a press agency. "Mother Teresa? This is the editor of the agency. The Philippine government has just awarded you the Magsaysay Prize. Heartfelt compliments! It involves a considerable sum."

Mother Teresa: "Thanks for letting me know."

The editor: "What do you plan on doing with the 50,000 rupees from the prize?" Mother Teresa: "What did you say? 50,000 rupees? I think the Lord wants us to build a home for children at Agra."

The Catholic Church too has a high regard for the work of Mother Teresa and her Sisters. This was shown by the decision of Pope Paul VI to assign the John XXIII Prize for Peace to Mother Teresa.

At the ceremony when this award was made on January 6, 1971, the then Secretary of State, Cardinal Villot, in the presence of the pope, of many cardinals, bishops and other eminent personalities, addressed her in these words:

"It was rather difficult to select one person from among so many people and organizations which have distinguished themselves in doing good to their fellow human beings. But we decided on Mother Teresa Bojaxhiu, the foundress of the Missionaries of Charity in Calcutta, who during her whole life has dedicated herself to the service of the poorest, to soothing the bitterest sufferings, and showing mercy to the greatest misfortunes."

On this occasion the Secretary General of the United Nations, Mr. U Thant, sent to the Vatican the following telegram:

"Keeping in mind what I know about Mother Teresa and her work, I feel that this award is worthy of the name of your holiness' great predecessor, John XXIII, whose goodness and generosity were so well known all over the world."

In reference to this ceremony, Mother Teresa told us with a smile at Oslo, on the eve of the day in 1979 when she was given the Nobel Peace Prize:

"When I was supposed to receive the Pope John XXIII Prize in Rome, all my Sisters had tickets to get in, but I had none; so when it came to my turn the guards stopped me, and did not want to let me go in without permission. I did not know what to do; but fortunately there came along a bishop who recognized me, and explained everything to the sentinel. The latter fell silent, then blushed, and then very politely and with many words, asked me to forgive him. It was only thanks to that bishop that I was able to receive the award!"

The ceremony took place in the presence of the entire diplomatic corps accredited to the Holy See, of some fifteen cardinals, and many bishops, monsignors and other dignitaries.

But the prize winner herself had come to the Vatican on the city bus, and was wearing her Indian *sari*, worth about one dollar.

In September 1971, she received at Boston another award, the "Good Samaritan" award.

The citation read: "In presenting this prize to Mother Teresa we wish to give due recognition to her efforts to alleviate the misery of the poor and needy in the world. Her work is an inspiration for others, and affords a marvelous example of how to take care of human beings. With this Good Samaritan Prize we wish to present her example in bold relief."

In Washington, on October 16, 1971, she received the John F. Kennedy award, which was accompanied by this citation: "In her unique geography of mercy Mother Teresa knows where she should live, and in her exemplary faith she never doubts whether she will have the means to do so. We feel honored in being able to declare that her trust is constantly and abundantly rewarded."

The prize money given her on this occasion was used to build a home for handicapped children north of Calcutta, at Dum-Dum, near Green Park.

On October 29, 1971, at the University of Washington, in the presence of all the faculty, professors and students, Mother Teresa was awarded an honorary doctorate in sociology, because "she has demonstrated by all her life and work how solutions can be found for the social problems which today afflict most of humanity."

Another testimonial to the esteem in which India holds the work of Mother Teresa was the award presented to her by the government at New Delhi on November 15, 1972. Dr. Giri, the president of India, in an inspired discourse, spoke of her, calling her "an angel of mercy" because she has restored to people the hope in life which they had lost.

"Today we honor a soul close to God, a woman who interprets Christian love through her good works. I am an optimist, and am convinced that so long as there are people like Mother Teresa, humanity can live in hope."

Speaking of the works of the Missionaries of Charity which are already a legend on various continents, President Giri said: "There can be no better contribution to human brotherhood than an activity as solid and opportune as theirs."

The Committee for Cultural Affairs motivated the prize with these words: "One rarely sees a sacrifice as disinterested and as unwearying as that of Mother Teresa, in favor of the weakest, the most miserable and unwanted members of human society. This altruistic service, performed without regard for nationality, caste, or religion, with no expectation of public acknowledgment, is a marvelous example of how a silent and effective task, an exhausting service, can contribute to the promotion of friendship and understanding among peoples."

At the award ceremony, besides President Giri, there were present Indira Gandhi, the daughter of Jawaharlal Nehru, vice president of the government, many ministers and other distinguished persons.

With her usual simplicity, and with a smile on her lips, Mother Teresa on this occasion somewhat moved, made a beautiful speech the main points of which were:

"What do my Brothers and Sisters and our collaborators do all over the world? They labor for the welfare of others; they proclaim their love of God. Those who came to help us work with the Bengalese refugees told us that they had received much more from those whom they had come to serve than they themselves had given. So you see, each one of us proves the same thing: our people need this, especially. Think of the babies abandoned without love. One day I saw one little fellow who did not want to eat. His mother was already dead. I found his sister, who looked most like him, and told her to go and play with him. His appetite returned almost at once, and he got better."

She also spoke of the leper problem. It is a terrible disease, but even worse is the feeling these people have of being repelled by their own families.

To all those present, without flinching, she posed the question:

"What has India done for her four million lepers?"

Her talk moved everyone, especially Mrs. Gandhi. Mother Teresa closed by saying: "Only you and I together can quench the thirst for love that burns in the hearts of all these people."

The Minister for Foreign Trade, Mr. George, also spoke:

"Mother Teresa has taught us what it means to love. This modest, frail little woman came from thousands of miles away to dedicate her life to the inhabitants of the poor regions of Calcutta. While she was speaking she had no prepared text to read from. Standing at the microphone she had nothing but her heart. She simply told us about the causes which make the hearts of people suffer: the idea that they are neither loved nor wanted."

When Mother Teresa praised the work of her Sisters, Indira Gandhi wept with emotion and thanked her.

Another prize was awarded to her for "the promotion of faith in the world." It was presented on April 25, 1973, in London, by Prince Philip of Edinburgh, in the presence of Queen Elizabeth II of England. On this occasion Prince Philip declared: "When I found who was being awarded the prize I thought that Mr. Templeton would agree with me in saying that Mother Teresa has given to this prize a new meaning. . . . Today we view with admiration her life and works, and we thank her for having brought all of us together here to meditate on all of this. The goodness which has shone on the world thanks to Mother Teresa can make us humble, lead us to marvel, and inspire enthusiasm. What more is there to say when her works themselves speak of her? I do not know what to say; I do not dare speak of Mother Teresa.

"She draws all her strength from God. She was nurtured in the faith in her family home: a home with a Christian tradition; in her family, a true Christian community; there she came to understand love and divine mercy. Then she forged for herself an experience of a similar task. I hope that her example and teaching may become the means by which Christian ideals may appear clear and living to a great many persons."

Mother Teresa thanked Prince Philip and all those present at the beautiful, simple ceremony.

"My dear co-workers, let us thank God that Mr. Templeton with a courageous gesture, has shared with us the wealth which God has given him, for His own glory and honor, and for the good of his brethren. The prize has been given to me, but it belongs to all those who cooperate in this work of love everywhere in the world. Some time ago a man came to me and said: 'I will give you most of what I have if someone will only come to visit me now and then. I am getting blind; my wife suffers from depression; my children are scattered about the world. We are dying of loneliness.'

"At Melbourne I visited an old man who nobody thought was still alive. I noticed that the room was untidy, and I began to clean it up. He interrupted me at once: 'Leave it alone; I like it like that.' I did not answer him, and in the end he gave in. In the room there was a very pretty lamp, but it was covered with dust. I asked him, 'Why don't you light it?' He answered: 'Why should I, and for whom? Nobody ever comes here, so it's of no use to me.' I asked him, 'If the Sisters came, would you turn it on?' 'Yes,' he said, 'if I only heard the sound of a human voice.'

"Some time later I received this message: 'Tell my friend that the lamp she lighted in my life is still burning.'

"We must all know people like that. When we know them we can cure them and help them.

"We cannot be satisfied with just giving them money. Money is not enough. Money can be given, but what they need even more is your hands, to serve them, your heart to love them.

"The first time I went out into the London streets it was cold, but there were still lots of people about. I met an old man, fairly well dressed, but shivering with cold. Another man was covering him with his own coat, when the other told him: 'Take me with you, wherever you want to go, but find me a bed where I can sleep.'

"If one wants to be another Jesus, he must be like the real one, who says in holy scripture: 'I sought someone to help me, but found none.' How sad it would be if today Christ had to say the same thing about us!'

"Christ is making use of me as a means for uniting people. Of this I have become convinced wherever I go. People tend to get together because all need God."

This was the first time that the Templeton Prize was awarded, and the jury had to select from among two thousand candidates the one who would receive the 34,000 pounds sterling. The jury was composed of ten persons belonging to different religions: two Anglicans, two Presbyterians, one Methodist, one Jew, one Moslem, one Buddhist monk, a Hindu, and a Catholic.

That same year she received at Los Angeles the St. Louise de Marillac Prize, named in honor of the foundress of the Sisters of Charity of St. Vincent.

In 1974 she also received, again in the United States, the Mater et Magistra Prize from the Third Order of St. Francis of Assisi, while at the Catholic University of St. Francis Xavier, conducted by the Jesuits, she was given an honorary doctorate.

The United Nations World Organization for the war on hunger, the Food and Agriculture Organization (FAO) on the occasion of its jubilee, in the Holy Year 1975, coined a medal having on one side the figure of Ceres holding a spear of wheat, in honor of Mother Teresa; the inscription reads: Mother Teresa—Ceres, FAO Rome; on the reverse, near the figure of a starving baby to whom two hands are offering a bowl of food, we find the inscription: Food for All; Holy Year 1975.

This award was made to her by the Director General of the FAO, Edward Faoum, "because of her exemplary conduct towards the starving and the poorest of this world." The money realized from the sale of these medals went to the support of her institute.

That same year she took part, as the envoy of Pope Paul VI, in the world conference on women, in Mexico. Again, in the same year, she received in California the Albert Schweitzer Prize, established in honor of the great humanist and Christian missionary, who won the Nobel Peace Prize in 1952, and who lived from 1875 to 1965.

The University of Santiniketan-Visva-Bharati decided in 1976 to confer on her an honorary degree. On departing for the Indian capital, she declared: "I am going to Santiniketan to receive an honorary doctorate. I do not understand why the universities and colleges keep giving me honorary degrees. Each time, I am undecided whether to go or not. These mean nothing to me. These are really only occasions to speak to people who perhaps have never heard of Jesus."

The award was made by the head of the Indian government, at the time Ms. Indira Gandhi.

She also got an honorary degree from one of the most famous institutions in the world, the University of Cambridge. The ceremony took place on June 10, 1977 in the aula magna of the university. Once again the degree was conferred on her by Prince Philip of Edinburgh, husband of Queen Elizabeth II. He stated: "It may be that the conferring of an honorary degree is not of any great utility. But how else can a university show its esteem and admiration for persons who, in its opinion, make a significant contribution to human culture? Besides, it is the task of a university to cultivate better knowledge and mutual understanding among peoples, by honoring those who accomplish this role with conspicuous success."

When they made her put on the long, silken Doctor's gown, with a long mantle over it, her *sari* disappeared, and on the floor one could see only her sandals, with her fragile, nude feet in them.

On March 1, 1979, she received 250,000,000 lire for her contributions to "humanity, peace and brotherhood among peoples."

This award, called the International Balzan Prize after the name of the international organization sponsoring it, was presented to her by the president of the Italian republic, Mr. Sandro Pertini. On this occasion Pope John Paul II received her in a private audience.

That day a journalist asked her what she intended to do with the money. She answered: "I shall use it mainly for the leprosy center."

On July 16 of that same year she received in Philadelphia in the presence of Cardinal Krol, an honorary doctorate from Temple University, the fifth award of this kind, and the second one in the United States.

In the fall of that same year a surprise was awaiting her and all the world: The Nobel Peace Prize.

The Nobel Peace Prize

When in October 1979 word began spreading that the Norwegian Nobel Committee had chosen to give the Peace Prize to Mother Teresa of Calcutta, there was great excitement everywhere in the world.

When the news first reached her, Mother Teresa declared:

"I personally am not worthy of it. I shall accept it in the name of the poor, because I think that the Committee, in awarding the prize to me, has wished to recognize the existence of the poor in the world. . . . But what is this? Only a drop compared with the ocean of suffering in this world."

In the world press. . .

For a long time the figure and the example of Mother Teresa and of her Missionaries of Charity have filled the pages of the world press, not only the religious press, but also numberless newspapers, reviews and publications of all kinds. We can say that there is no newspaper which did not speak about her, especially after the reception of the Nobel Peace Prize in 1979.

Here are just a few short excerpts:

"The singular activity of Mother Teresa is worthy of the highest praise, for she has dedicated some thirty years to the welfare of humanity, in which God alone knows how many thousands and perhaps millions of persons die of need" (*London Guardian*).

"She is not a political figure. She believes in God and with all her strength she seeks to help those in wretched living conditions" (*Die Welt,* Hamburg).

"The Nobel Peace Prize for this year has been awarded to one who has labored all her life helping others, restoring hope to them and liberating them from misery, while respecting and loving each one of them without concern for their social class or position" (*Verdens Gang,* Oslo).

"The example of Mother Teresa has not remained sterile and unknown, but has obtained the great acknowledgment that goodness, love and respect for one's neighbor, as well as for the dignity of human life, are basic values. The Nobel Committee, by recognizing these values as the sole path to peace, is, in fact, grateful to her for the outstanding results she has obtained" (*Toronto Star*).

"Mother Teresa was typically herself when, on accepting the Nobel Peace Prize, she said, 'I did not deserve it.' Such a declaration is not only a sign of personal humility, but also of her basic conviction and attitude: that by serving and helping the poor she is in fact merely doing her duty, which is in addition the duty of us all" (*New York Times*).

"She affirms that the worst affliction of all is not leprosy or TB, but the feeling of not being wanted, of not being loved, of not having anybody who cares about you. The poorest of the poor are the children of Mother Teresa" (*Newsweek,* New York).

"The prize given to Mother Teresa is just, because it helps to proclaim peace and international understanding among people. As all know, hunger, poverty and indifference are the great danger for peace in the world" (*El Sol,* Mexico City).

"Her only desire is that all the sick, the infirm, the poor, and all who suffer injustice may live in peace, or that at least a death with dignity may give them back their human worth" (*Tagesanzeiger,* Bern).

"Her example of total devotedness in the struggle against human misery and her courage stimulate thousands of men and women to do something in favor of those great ideals. Her charitable missionary work was transformed since 1950, when it evolved, and still is evolving, into an institution in the service of the poor, in India and elsewhere" (*Indian Express,* New Delhi).

"In truth, this year the Committee for awarding the Nobel Peace Prize has succeeded remarkably well. It is good to discover that the world still recognizes virtue, that hope and love can still overcome cynicism and misery. . . . Today humanity sees in her something different from others, because it restores to man some faith in himself" (*Times of India,* New Delhi).

"It is good that in the International Year of the Child such recognition should be made, because her work and care for children is known to all. It has become proverbial. In her charitable work and in her life we can find many other fields of interest and in other places, but Calcutta remains the center of her activity. The fact that Mother Teresa has received the Nobel Peace Prize is a motive of joy for all India, the country which she has adopted as her third homeland" (*Amrita Bazar Patrika,* Calcutta).

"These lines are dedicated to the woman who has spent her whole life among the most needy. . . . Her work is only a part of her life in which we find crises and glories, mingled in a strange and marvelous manner" (*Hindustan Times,* New Delhi).

"Rarely, in fact almost never before, has this honor been greeted so unanimously and deservedly as it was this year, when it was decided to give the Nobel Peace Prize to Mother Teresa of Calcutta" (*The Statesman,* New Delhi).

"The Nobel Committee has proved its own capacity by choosing Mother Teresa for this year's Peace Prize" (*Ananda Bazar Patrika,* Calcutta).

"Mother Teresa is so close to holiness that people of these times can scarcely imagine it. Her work has surpassed all the efforts and the aims of all those who labor for peace" (*The Tribune,* Chandrigarh).

"Mother Teresa has become a living saint, a legend even during her lifetime, because she has dedicated her all to the service of the most miserable, to those who most need understanding and love" (*Deccan Herald,* Bangalore).

The Indian government

On the occasion of the awarding of the Prize to Mother Teresa, the Indian government organized an official reception on November 9, 1979. The entire government was on hand, led by the Prime Minister, the Minister for Foreign Affairs, and many other distinguished guests. A sumptuous banquet had been prepared, but Mother Teresa refused to attend, saying: "I could not take part and eat all that food with a clear conscience, knowing how many of my brothers and sisters even today are dying of hunger. All I need is a piece of bread and a glass of water."

At the start she was greeted by the Prime Minister, Charan Singh:

"Mother Teresa came to India fifty years ago. Her choice was a happy one for our country. In India alone she takes care of 56,000 lepers and, in addition, of a great number of poor and neglected people. It would take a Shakespeare or a Milton to describe her achievements in India. Her manner of serving humanity is truly incomparable."

Here is a summary of Mother Teresa's talk:

"India is my homeland. By awarding me the Nobel Prize the world has given recognition to a work of love and peace."

"Gandhi said something very beautiful: 'Whoever serves the poor serves God.' Our people need not our compassion, but our mercy and love.

"Love and assistance, although they are an end in themselves, have their reward. By serving I have received much more than I gave. I beseech you to give to the poor of your abundance, to give of your love till it hurts. The poor are very gentle people. We humiliate them if we think that they are poor, and that's all. We do not know them, and so we do not love them.

"I get the impression that people accept abortion out of fear of having children. They are afraid that they will have to feed one more child. I beg you in this International Year of the Child, to avert this dreadful curse. God will provide enough food for his children. Doing away with abortion would be a great blessing in this year."

After her refusal to attend the gala banquet, other guests followed her example, so that the banquet was cancelled and the food distributed to the poor. At the end of the meeting Mother Teresa thanked everyone most cordially and said that she had to go to be with her dying patients, and that she had no more time to spend with the guests since she had work to do. Then there took place something never before seen in India. Here is how she herself described what happened.

"The Indian government—all the ministers with the Prime Minister leading—after I had turned down the big banquet, spontaneously came to our house for the dying, caressed them with their own hands, and greeted them. This was something really incredible in India; for great and famous personages to come and visit the lepers and the dying. Something really phenomenal, beyond anything that could have been imagined or expected. You cannot believe what it means, for people with this mentality. The patients were out of themselves, and could not credit what was happening, could not imagine that so many high ranking people were really among them. God is preparing something great for our people, for us all, and for the world. I am firmly convinced of this."

The awarding of the Peace Prize

The day of the feast of the Immaculate Conception, December 8, 1979, was a very beautiful one. It seemed almost summerlike in Oslo, with the special luminous northern sun. Oslo, the Norwegian capital, was decorated as for a feast day; many pictures of Mother Teresa, and words praising her hung in the windows and on the walls. In front of the St. Joseph Institute where we lodged, and where Mother Teresa and her

133

Sisters also lived, a huge Norwegian flag waved gently, as a sign of welcome for the occasion, as we shall relate below.

About 3:30 P.M. the Oslo airport became the center of attention for the journalists from all over the world, and for the crowd as well. The door of the plane opened, and with a light but sure step "the angel in an Indian *sari*, the white angel of peace" emerged, smiling and unruffled as ever. She was welcomed by the president of the Norwegian Nobel Committee, John Sanness, then by the other members of the Committee, and by the clerical representatives: Bishop Gran of Oslo, our own Bishop Nikola Prela, and many others.

In the press room an interview was organized. Questions were put to her first by the journalists of the British Broadcasting Corporation, then by those from various American stations, then those from the Scandinavian countries, from Italian Radiotelevision, and many more. The questions covered hunger, peace, and justice in the world. To one journalist she answered directly: "You and I must work for peace; it is a duty for us, for all people. The most powerful weapon for achieving peace is love, and living for God."

For the reviews *Drita* and *Kana* I also asked a question: "Mother Teresa, you are a child of the Albanian people and you come from our diocese of Skopje and Prizren. What can you tell us and our readers, who follow your activity faithfully and with love, especially during these last ten years? What message have you for the people of Albania and Yugoslavia?"

She replied: "Tell them to love one another, to bring prayer back into their homes; for wherever there is prayer people can live in peace and mutual love."

After the press conference, Mother Teresa went to the Indian embassy, which was also crowded with people.

December 10 was the day of the actual awarding of the Prize.

"About 12:30 Mother Teresa, in a special limousine with an honor guard proceeded to the university auditorium where the great honor was to be conferred on her. The adjacent square was filled with people who, with joyful shouts, each in his or her own way, greeted the 'Mother of Peace.' We entered the hall. There followed long and cordial applause. At 12:50

134

King Olaf V of Norway entered with his suite, and five minutes later the ceremony began, with the participation of the head of the Norwegian government, the ministers, the diplomatic corps, representatives of the world of culture, and the journalists. Norwegian radio and television broadcast the entire ceremony, which was retransmitted in Eurovision and by other networks. The address in the name of the Nobel Committee was made by its president, John Sanness, who brought out "the spirit of the doctrine of Mother Teresa."

After this Mother Teresa, from the "chair of peace" began her great "hour-long lesson on peace in the world." She spoke of various world problems, the role of woman in the family and in society, divorce, abortion, the problem of poverty and injustice, and then of love and peace in the world. "The poor are not looking for our pity, nor for our sympathy. They need our love which will understand them and accept them."

There then took place the solemn presentation of the prize: a gold medal and a special diploma, together with a considerable sum of money as a gift for the works of peace. We all stood and applauded with enthusiasm. The first to congratulate her was the King and his family; then the members of the Nobel Committee, and various personalities. Mother Teresa, short as she is, remained almost invisible, surrounded by her many friends. Finally there was sung a hymn of thanksgiving by J. S. Bach.

In front of the university hall there were other demonstrations by the crowd, amid general enthusiasm. The procession advanced slowly towards the Continental Hotel, for a modest cocktail, since as we have mentioned, Mother Teresa had declined the customary gala banquet in favor of ;he poor.

At the end of this festive day, especially dear to those who struggle for peace, justice and the well being of others, Mother Teresa went to visit the Yugoslav embassy at Oslo. She was welcomed by the ambassador who said: "In the name of our country I congratulate Mother Teresa for this high honor she has received. Like congratulations have been sent to her by President Tito, one of the first to felicitate her on winning the Nobel Peace Prize, given her for her work and for her humanitarian mission. I believe, as many others have already said, that this year the Prize was awarded to a person who richly deserved it because of what she has accomplished, and because of the love which she shows in it."

After this she answered a few questions from the Yugoslav journalists and for the listeners to Radio Pristina. She stated, in Albanian, "I always keep our Albanian people in my heart. I beg the Lord that his peace may fill our hearts, our families and all the world. Pray much for my poor people, and I too will pray for you. God bless you all!"

When we came back to St. Josseph's, more work and more interviews were awaiting her. When it was all over that evening she said: "I am used to working day and night, often till midnight and sometimes later, but I just can't get used to all this. . . ." She thus made us understand in her own way how exhausted she was.

Mother Teresa's speech at the prize awarding ceremony

"Since we are gathered here to thank God for the granting of the Nobel Peace Prize, I think it would be appropriate to recite St. Francis' prayer, which never fails to move me. We say it every day after holy communion, because it fits each one of us. It always makes me happy to know that even 450 years ago when St. Francis composed it, the world faced the same difficulties we face today, and that the prayer is, therefore, so up to date. I think that some of you already know it, and so we can recite it together.

"Let us thank God for the occasion which brings us together today, for the gift of peace which reminds us that we were created to live in this peace, that Jesus became a man to bring the good news to the poor. He, God, became a man, in all things like unto us except sin, and he clearly declared that he had come to bring us this good news.

"This good news was peace for all people of good will, and this is what we desire: peace in our hearts. God loved the world so much that he gave us his Son—a great gift indeed. We can say that the gift of the sufferings of his Son given to us by God comes from his love for the world. He gave him to the

Virgin Mary, and how did she react? No sooner had he become incarnate in her than she hastened to proclaim the good news; and no sooner had she reached her cousin Elizabeth's house than the child not yet born, the son of Elizabeth, leaped for joy. That little unborn child was the first herald of peace. He recognized Christ, he recognized that Christ had come to bring the good news to me and to you. And as though it did not suffice that he should become man, he died on the cross to show his love more clearly still. He died for you, for me, for the leper, for the starving, for the ones living naked in the streets, not only of Calcutta, but also in Africa, in New York, Oslo, London . . . asking us to love one another as he has loved us. In the gospel we read: 'Love each other as I have loved you; as the Father loved me so do I love you.' As the Father loved him . . . and so he gave him to us; and as we love one another we should give ourselves to one another, even unto suffering.

"One cannot say, 'Love God, not your neighbor.' St. John calls liars those who pretend to love God but do not love their neighbor. How can we love the God whom we do not see if we do not love our fellow human being whom we do see? Whom we can touch? With whom we live? It is important to realize that love, to be genuine must bring some suffering with it.

"Jesus too suffered in order to love us. He still suffers. To be sure that we might remember his great love he became our bread of life to satisfy our hunger for his love, our hunger for God, because it was for this love that we were created. We were created to love and to be loved, and he became man to enable us to love him as he loves us. He has become one with the hungry, the naked, the homeless, the sick, the persecuted, the lonely, the abandoned ones; and he tells us: 'You made me like this.' He hungers for our love, and this is the hunger that afflicts our poor people. This is the hunger that every one of us ought to seek out. It might even be found in our own homes.

"I can never forget the day when I was visiting a hospital where there were elderly parents whose children had contented themselves with placing them in the hospital, and after that had more or less forgotten about them. I went there and saw that there were many pretty things in the place; but all the eyes were fixed on the door. Nobody smiled. I turned to my Sisters and asked: 'Why? Why are these people, who have everything they need here, always looking towards the door? Why do none of them smile?'

"I am accustomed to seeing a smile on the face of our people, even those who are dying. They answered me: 'It is like this every day. They wait and hope that a son or daughter may come to visit them. They suffer because they have been forgotten.' You see, love is what they need. Poverty exists even in our homes, the poverty which means a lack of affection. Perhaps in our own family someone feels alone, sick, worried; and these are difficult times for all. But are we present? Are we ready to accept these folks? Does a mother know how to welcome a son?

"I was amazed when I learned that in the West so many young people are on drugs. I tried to understand the reason for this. Why? The answer is, 'because in the family there is nobody who cares about them.' Fathers and mothers are so busy they have no time. Young parents work, and the child lives in the street, and goes his own way. We speak of peace. These are the things that threaten peace. I think that today peace is threatened by abortion too, which is a true war, the direct killing of the child by its own mother. In the Bible we read that God clearly said: 'Even though a mother did forget her infant, I will not forget him.'

"Today, abortion is the worst evil, and the greatest enemy of peace. We who are here today were wanted by our parents. We would not be here if our parents had not wanted us.

"We want children, and we love them. But what about the other millions? Many are concerned about the children, like those in Africa, who die in great numbers either from hunger or for other reasons. But millions of children die intentionally, by the will of their mothers. This is what is destroying peace today. Because if a mother can kill her own child, what will prevent us from killing ourselves, or one another? Nothing.

"Here is what I beg for in India, what I pray for everywhere. 'Let us turn once again to the children.' And since this is the 'Year of the Child' I ask: 'What have we done for them?' At the start of the year I said and repeated everywhere: 'Let us see that this year every child may be born, and that the ones who aren't wanted may be wanted. Have children really been wanted this year?'

"Let me tell you something that is truly frightening. We combat abortion with adoption and thus save thousands of lives. We spread the word in all the clinics, hospitals, police stations: 'We beg you not to kill the children; we will take them.' At all hours of the day and of the night—among us there are many unmarried mothers—someone calls and we say: 'Come in, we will take care of you and your baby; we will give it a home.' There are also a large number of families without any children. This too is a divine blessing for us. And we again do something useful. We teach the natural method of family planning to our beggars, lepers, to the inhabitants of the slums, and the street dwellers.

"In just six years in Calcutta (all this refers to Calcutta) we had 61,273 fewer babies than might have been born if the families, instead of self-control had practiced other methods, without true love. Many times people have told me: 'Now our family is healthy, united, and we have a child when we want one.' I think that if this is possible for these street people, these beggars, it ought to be possible for all the rest who know ways and means of not destroying the life that God has created in us.

"The poor are good people. They can teach us much. One day a man came to thank us: 'You who practice chastity have taught us very well how to plan our family, because self-control is nothing but love of one for the other.' I think he was right. And many times these are people who have nothing to eat, nor a house to live in, yet they know how to be great.

"The poor are wonderful people. One evening we picked up four in the street; one was in pitiful condition. I told the other Sisters: 'You take care of the other three; I will see about this weakest one.' I did all that my love enabled me to do: I put her in a bed, and on her face there appeared a marvelous smile. She took my hand, and after saying just one word: 'Thanks!' she died.

"I could not help examining my conscience before her. I asked myself: 'What would I have done had I been in her place?' The answer was easy. I would have tried to attract attention; I would have said: 'I am dying; I am hungry; I am cold; it hurts;' or something of the sort. Instead, she gave me much more than I had given her: love with gratitude. She died with a smile on her lips, like the man we pulled out of a canal, half devoured by worms, and whom we took to our house. 'I used to live like a beast in the streets,' he murmured; 'now I am going to die like an angel, loved and cared for.' It was something beautiful to see the humanity of this man who spoke thus, and who died without any rancor towards anyone, without cursing anyone, without self pity. Yes, like an angel; like most of our people.

"That is why we believe what Jesus said: 'I was hungry, naked, homeless, unwanted, hated, nobody cared about me . . . and you did this for me!'

"I don't think we are really social workers. Perhaps in the eyes of people we seem to be such. But we are contemplatives in the world's heart. For we touch the body of Jesus twenty-four hours a day. We spend all those hours in his presence, and so do you. You should seek to gather together the spirit of your family because the family that prays remains together. I think that we in our families do not need bombs and guns to destroy or to bring peace, but only to be united, to love one another, to bring peace and joy, a greater reciprocal considera-tion in our homes. We could overcome all the evils of the world. There is so much suffering, so much hate, so much misery; and to remedy this we must start in our homes with prayers and sacrifices. Love is born in homes because the important thing is not what we do, but with how much love we do it. It depends on almighty God, hence what we do is not important, since God is immense; but on us depends the love we put into our work, in what we do for him in the people we serve.

"There was a time in Calcutta when it was very difficult for us to get any sugar. I don't know how this came to the ears of the children, but a little four-year-old went home and said to his parents: 'I don't want to eat any sugar for three days; I want to give it to Mother Teresa.' Three days later his father and mother came to our house with the little fellow. I had never seen them before, and the child could hardly pronounce my name. But he knew very well why he had come: to share his love with others.

"That is why I receive so much love everywhere. When I got here I was surrounded with love, real love, love full of understanding. It was as though all those in Asia, in Africa, were really close by. I feel at home here as though I had been speaking with my Sisters today; as though I were still in the convent in Calcutta. I really feel this.

"So today I speak to you and want you to try to look for the poor, first in your own house, and there begin with love. Be the good news for your loved ones. Take interest in your neighbors. Do you know who are your neighbors?

"I got a good lesson from a Hindu family with eight children. The man came to me and said: 'Mother, there is a family with eight children who have nothing to eat. Do something!' I took some rice and went to see about them. I saw the children with eyes dulled by hunger. I don't know whether you have ever seen hunger; I have, often. The woman accepted the rice, divided it up, and left the house. When she came back I asked her, 'Where did you go, and what did you do?' She answered simply: 'They were hungry too.' What impressed me the most was that she was aware of it. And who were 'they'? A Moslem family. I did not give them any more rice that evening, because I wanted them to be able to savor their own gift. But the children were all happy, sharing the joy of their mother who had been able to make a gift of love. You see where love is born in the home. I was most grateful too for what I had received. This has been a wonderful experience for me here in Oslo. I shall go back to India where I hope to remain until the fifteenth, and I shall be able to bring them your love.

"I know very well that you did not give only out of your abundance, but that you have given until it hurts. Today even the children have given something. I was much surprised to learn that such is the joy of the starving little ones, because for them they need love, along with all the rest they get from their parents.

"So, let us thank God for having had the chance of knowing each other and of drawing closer to each other. We will be able to help the children of the whole world because, as you know, the Sisters are all over the world. And with this prize which I have received as a prize for peace I shall try to build a home for those who have none. For I believe that love is born in a home; and if you could visit a house of poor people, love would grow even greater. First come the poor in your own home, then in your own country, then in the world. To be able to do this our Sisters' lives must be filled with prayer. They need to be drenched with Christ in order to understand, to want to share. Today there is so much suffering, and I feel that the passion of Christ is beginning all over again. We share in that passion, in the sufferings of the people, and not only in the poor countries. I have found in the West a poverty very difficult to eliminate.

"When I help a hungry person I send him or her off with a plate of rice and a piece of bread. But the marginalized, the rejected, the unloved, the persons estranged from society endure a very bitter lot, a poverty difficult to bear. In the West the Sisters work with such people.

"So, pray with us that we may be the Good News. We cannot do this without your help. You should do this here, in your own country. You must recognize the poor. Perhaps here people are materially well off, but I think if we looked inside the houses we should find that it is difficult sometimes to smile at each other, even though such a smile might be the beginning of love.

"For this reason we always greet each other with a smile, because it is the beginning of love, and when one begins to love it is natural to want to do something. So pray for our Sisters, for me, for our Brothers, for our co-workers in the whole world. Pray so that we may remain faithful to God's gift, faithful in loving him in the poor, along with you. All we do would be impossible without your prayer, your gifts, your continual help. But I do not want you to give me what you have left over; I want you to give me all, even the suffering.

"Some time ago I received fifteen dollars from a man who for the past twenty years has been unable to move at all except for his right hand. His only pleasure was smoking. He told me: 'I haven't smoked for a week, and here is the money I saved.'

That must have been a big sacrifice for him, but how beautiful it is! With the money I bought some bread and gave it to those who were hungry; it was happiness for both; he gave, and the poor accepted.

"This is something we can do, you and I. It is a gift of God that we can share, this love for others. And the ability to do it comes to us from Jesus. Let us love one another as he loved us. Let us love him with a single love. Now that Christmas is coming, let us share the joy of loving him and of loving one another.

"Let us keep the joy of loving Jesus in our hearts, and let us share it with all those we meet. To spread that joy is real, because Christ is in us. Christ is in our hearts, in the others we meet, in the smiles we give and receive. Let us do the essential: that not one single child may be unwanted, that we may meet each other and smile, especially when it is hard to smile.

"I remember that once there came to our house in Calcutta fourteen professors from various American universities. We arranged for them to visit our house for the dying. In that house we have had over 36,000 patients gathered up from the streets of Calcutta, and among them 18,000 died peacefully. They went to the house of the Lord. When these men arrived we began to speak about love and mercy towards one another. One of them asked me: 'Mother, tell us something to remember.' And I said: 'Smile at one another; dedicate yourselves to each other, to your families; smile at one another.'

"Another man asked me: 'Are you married?' I told him: 'Yes, and sometimes it is difficult for me to smile at Jesus, because he is very hard to please.' That is really true. Love is always needed, when it is required, and when we suffer with joy.

"As I have already said today, if I do not go to heaven for anything else, it will be for this publicity, because it purifies me, obliges me to sacrifice, and prepares me for paradise.

"I think I am living a good life. Jesus is with us and loves us. If we would only remember how much he loves us and if we began again to love each other as he loves us, not in the big things only but in the little ones as well, Norway would become a haven of love. How beautiful it would be if it became the center from which peace would flow! If from here salvation would arise for the unborn. If it became the flame of peace igniting the world; then the Nobel Peace Prize would be the gift of the Norwegians. God bless you!"